CYPRUS
1946-68

Edited by Hal Kosut

FACTS ON FILE, INC.   NEW YORK

CYPRUS 1946-68

Library of Congress Catalog Card Number: 70-130641

ISBN 0-87196-183-0

9   8   7   6   5   4   3   2   1

CONTENTS

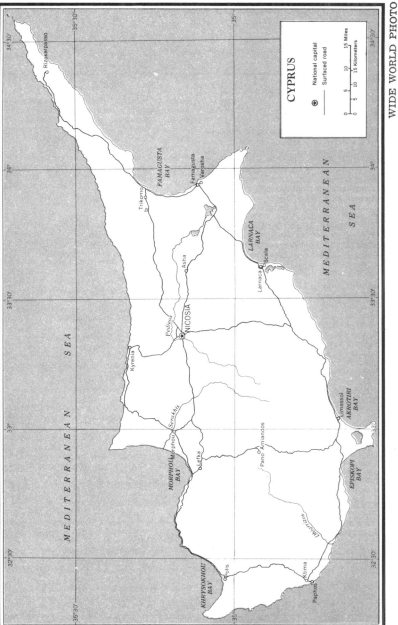

CYPRUS

⊕ National capital
— Surfaced road

0 5 10 15 Miles
0 5 10 15 Kilometers

M E D I T E R R A N E A N   S E A

Rizokarpasso

FAMAGUSTA BAY

Trikomo

Famagusta
Varosha

Asha

LARNACA BAY

Scala

Larnaca

NICOSIA

Pedieos

Kyrena

Serrakhis

Morphou

MORPHOU BAY

Lefka

Pano Amiandos

Limassol

AKROTIRI BAY

M E D I T E R R A N E A N   S E A

EPISKOPI BAY

KHRYSOKHOU BAY

Polis

Ktima

Paphos

Dhiarizos

BACKGROUND

CYPRUS IS A SMALL BUT STRATEGICALLY located island that has been ruled by well over a dozen foreign conquerors at various times during some 3,500 years of recorded history. Since the end of World War II, the violence battering this speck of land has been directed initially on winning independence from Great Britain but also on settling scores between Cypriots of Greek ancestry and Cypriots of Turkish origin.

The 3d largest island in the Mediterranean, Cyprus has an area of 3,572 square miles, including the small Cape Andreas (Klidhes) islands. It lies 44 miles south of Turkey, 60 miles west of Syria and 240 miles north of the United Arab Republic. The Troodos Massif in the southwest (highest peak — 6,400 feet) and the Kyrenia Mountains along the northern coast dominate the Cypriot landscape. The central plain of Mesaoria lies between these mountain ranges and stretches from Morphou Bay on the west to Famagusta Bay on the east.

The population of Cyprus as of 1970 totaled 621,000. About 79% of the population is of Greek ancestry; 18% is of Turkish origin. The remainder are Armenians, Maronites and members of other minority groups. Greek Cypriots largely belong to the autocephalous Orthodox Church of Cyprus whose primate, Archbishop Makarios III, is also secular leader (ethnarch) of the Greek Cypriot community and the first president of the republic. Virtually all Turkish Cypriots are Moslems. Although each of the 2 major ethnic groups speaks the language of its originating country, English is a quasi-*lingua franca* on Cyprus.

Turkish Cypriot settlements are scattered throughout the island and do not constitute a majority in any area of Cyprus. Significant numbers of Turkish Cypriots, however, have been dislocated as a result of civil strife since Dec. 1963.

Nicosia, the capital and the largest city of Cyprus, is located on the central plain and has a population of more than 90,000. Other important urban centers, all located on the coast, are: Limassol, Famagusta, Larnaca, Paphos, and Kyrenia.

Cyprus has been influenced predominantly by Greek culture. Political control has been exercised at various times by Phoenicians, Greeks, Assyrians, Macedonians, Egyptians, Persians, Romans, Byzantines, Saracens, Franks, Venetians, Genoese, Turks and British. The island was ruled by Turkey from 1571 to 1878, when British occupation and administration were substituted. Britain formally annexed Cyprus in 1914 at the outbreak of World War I, when Turkey was allied with the Central Powers, and the island became a crown colony in 1925 after Turkey conceded British sovereignty in the Treaty of Lausanne in 1923.

Since Greek independence in the early 19th century, Greek Cypriots had pressed for *enosis,* the union of Cyprus with Greece. Riots in 1931, led by supporters of *enosis,* resulted in the suspension of the Legislative Council by the British administration. In 1943 the British granted some autonomy to the island on the basis of male suffrage, and London pledged that self-government would be considered at the end of World War II. With the conclusion of the conflict, the Greek Cypriots began new political agitation for political independence. In 1954 Greece officially backed the Greek Cypriot claim to self-determination and supported the cause in UN debates. Turkey entered the dispute, contending that if Britain relinquished control over Cyprus, the island must be partitioned between Greek and Turkish Cypriots. Ankara held that a division of the island was vital to protect the security of Turkey and the Turkish Cypriot minority.

The impasse continued as British proposals for constitutional reform were deemed unacceptable by Greece and the Greek Cypriots. The controversy became acute in 1955 with the launching of a guerrilla campaign against the British by EOKA,

(National Organization for the Cyprus Struggle), the Greek Cypriot underground movement. The Turkish community resorted to violence in opposition to *enosis*. The following 4 years were marked by violence, increasing communal unrest and growing friction involving Britain, Greece and Turkey.

A major step toward resolving the Cyprus dispute was taken in Feb. 1959 when Greece, Turkey, Britain and the Greek and Turkish Cypriot communities signed agreements that led to the establishment of an independent Cyprus republic Aug. 16, 1960. Makarios became president. The orderly workings of the new government, however, were hampered by continued mutual suspicions of the 2 communities. The situation was further exacerbated by constitutional proposals submitted by Makarios in Nov. 1963 that imposed political restrictions on the Turkish Cypriots.

As tensions increased, armed strife broke out between the 2 communities in late Dec. 1963 and continued sporadically throughout 1963-7. Initially, a joint force composed of British, Greek and Turkish troops attempted to establish and enforce a cease-fire on the island. When this began to appear to be inadequate, the matter was referred to the UN Security Council. The Council, in a resolution of Mar. 4, 1964, established the UN Force in Cyprus (UNFICYP) and authorized the UN secretary general, in agreement with the parties, to designate a mediator to promote an agreed settlement. The force was authorized for an initial period of 3 months but has been extended at periodic intervals through 1970. It has maintained a UN presence on the island and has worked constantly to prevent minor incidents from developing into renewed fighting.

2 important individuals of Greek origin — Archbishop Makarios and Col. George Grivas — emerged during the early turbulence as the major leaders of the Greek Cypriot campaign for freedom:

Archbishop Makarios III, the outstanding figure in Cyprus' struggle for independence, was born Michael Christodouros

Archbishop Makarios III

Mouskos Aug. 13, 1913 in Ano Panyia in the Paphos district of Cyprus. He enrolled at the Kykko monastery of the Greek Orthodox Church at the age of 13. On becoming a monk, he assumed the name of Makarios, meaning "blessed." In 1938, only 2 years after completing his secondary education, Makarios became a deacon of the church and was later sent by the Kykko abbey to Greece to study at the Theological College of the University of Athens. Following his graduation in 1943, he returned to Cyprus to join the faculty of the abbey. In 1946 Makarios was ordained a priest in the Greek Orthodox Church. He went to the U.S. that year to advance his theological studies at the School of Theology of Boston University under a fellowship provided by the World Council of Churches. His election as metropolitan (bishop) of Kition in 1948 brought Makarios back to Cyprus to take up his new duties as religious leader in the districts of Limassol and Lanarca. On the death of Makarios II, in Oct. 1950, Makarios succeeded the prelate as archbishop and ethnarch, head of the Greek Orthodox Church of Cyprus.

As Cyprus' new religious leader, Makarios was pledged to support the plebiscite of Jan. 1950, in which 95% of the island's Greek Cypriots had voted in favor of *enosis*. Makarios began to engage actively in the drive for *enosis* in 1952. He pressed the claim at the UN General Assembly meeting in New York and in discussions with U.S. government officials in Washington. He enlisted the support of Greece to press his country's cause for self-determination at the UN in 1954. That year Makarios visited Paris and London to seek backing for the political struggle of the Greek Cypriots. In a further bid for international support, the archbishop attended the conference of non-aligned African-Asian countries in Bandung, Indonesia Aug. 29, 1954. Amid a rising tide of anti-British violence in Cyprus in 1955-6, Makarios held a series of negotiations with the British administrative authorities in a fruitless effort to find a solution to the dispute. Accused by the British of fomenting the disturbances, Makarios was deported to the Seychélle Islands in the Indian Ocean in Mar. 1956. He was released from detention the following year but was

forbidden to return to Cyprus. Makarios went to Greece instead
to carry on his political struggle. During his absence from
Cyprus, international efforts to resolve the crisis were pursued as
violence mounted.

Makarios joined British, Greek and Turkish officials in 1959
in negotiations that produced an agreement establishing an independent republic of Cyprus. Makarios returned to his native land
in Mar. 1959 and in Dec. 1959 was elected the first president of
Cyprus; he assumed the post on the declaration of the republic in
Aug. 1960. His rule during the following 8 years was marked by
intermittent political and military conflict with the Turkish
Cypriots, by confrontations with Turkey and by international
pressures aimed at preventing the dispute from erupting into a
regional conflict in the eastern Mediterranean. Makarios
tightened Greek Cypriot rule in 1965 by pushing through
electoral reforms that diminished the political power of the Turkish Cypriots. His presidential term expired in 1965 but was
extended twice by parliament because of continuing crises, and
he was reelected to a 2d 5-year term in 1968.

George Theodorus Grivas was born Mar. 23, 1898 in
Trikomo, in the Famagusta district of eastern Cyprus. After
attending elementary school in his native village, he enrolled in
1909 in the Pancyprian Gymnasium in Nicosia, a school for the
sons of leading Cypriot families. (Grivas' father was a well-to-do
merchant, and his mother was a physician.) On graduating in
1916, Grivas embarked on a military career by entering the
Royal Hellenic military academy in Athens. It was there that he
joined a Greek nationalist group pledged to a policy of *enosis.*
Grivas adopted Greek nationality after graduating from the
academy in 1919, and he joined the Greek infantry as a lieutenant. He fought for 6 months against the Turks in the 1922-3
Greek-Turkish Asia Minor campaign. In 1925 Grivas went to
France to advance his military career. He studied at the infantry
school in Versailles and at the fire-training school at Chalons-sur-
Marne. He was promoted to rank staff officer in the Greek army
in 1928. Grivas went back to France in 1932 to attend the Ecole
Superieure de la Guerre in Paris, and he graduated the following
year with distinction.

After the outbreak of World War II in 1939, Grivas was appointed to the operations office of the Greek army general staff. Following promotion to chief of staff of a division in Dec. 1940, he participated in the ill-fated Albanian campaign against the Italians. Grivas was later promoted to lieutenant colonel. Following Greece's military defeat and its occupation by German and Italian forces, Grivas joined an underground resistance group called "X." The group was one of several clandestine organizations that operated in occupied Athens and was composed mainly of rightwing and royalist army officers. As the Germans began evacuating Greece in 1944, Grivas' X organization shifted its military operations to action against the Communist-led guerrilla units in the mountains, which had battled the German occupiers. The fighting erupted into a full-scale civil war in the next 2 years. Grivas turned his attention to politics in 1946, and he transformed X into a rightwing pan-Hellenic party. He ran for parliament but was defeated, and he lost similar bids for a parliamentary seat in 1950 and 1951.

Grivas first entered the struggle for Cyprus' independence in 1952, when he arrived in the island to lay the groundwork for the creation of a guerrilla force that would eventually liberate the island from British colonial rule. He smuggled himself back into Cyprus in 1954 and started to organize his long-planned guerrilla army, the Ethniki Organosis Kyprion Agoniston (National Organization for the Cyprus Struggle), or EOKA. Grivas led EOKA in its first attack against British forces Apr. 1, 1955. EOKA, under his leadership, pressed the military struggle and violence against the British and also against the Turkish Cypriots for the next 4 years. Grivas assumed the aura of a legendary figure during this period; he adopted the *nomme de guerre* of Dighenis Akritas, a romantic Byzantine hero. Although he was the subject of an intense and widespread search by British security forces, Grivas managed to escape his pursuers. His true identity came to light in 1956 when British forces discovered photographs of him and documents attributed to him. After hostilities ended and the agreements of 1959 established an independent republic in Cyprus, Grivas came out of hiding from his clandestine EOKA headquarters in the Troodos Mountains and was granted safe-conduct to Greece.

Grivas resumed an active role in Cyprus' affairs after new violence erupted between the Greek and Turkish Cypriot communities in Dec. 1963. He returned to Cyprus in June 1964 as a self-styled peace-maker, and he sought to reconcile the divergent views among the Greek Cypriots on means of achieving a just solution of the dispute. In Aug. 1964 Grivas assumed command of the Greek Cypriot National Guard.

This book records the turbulent events of 1946-68 during which Cyprus won its independence but found its Greek and Turkish communities still at odds — and sometimes at war. The book's contents, like those of most INTERIM HISTORY volumes, are adapted largely from reports that appeared in FACTS ON FILE during the period covered plus such additional material from authentic sources as seems necessary.

Britain began political activity in 1946 to defuse growing unrest in Cyprus stemming from Greek Cypriot demands for an end to British rule. London's efforts were in the form of constitutional reforms aimed at giving the islanders greater self-rule. A series of similar charter proposals submitted through 1954 failed to satisfy the Greek Cypriots, who insisted that their ultimate goal remained enosis, union with Greece. The Turkish Cypriot minority, suspicious of Greek Cypriot dominance, favored continued British rule and accepted all the constitutional proposals.

Greece entered the political struggle in 1954 by submitting the Cyprus question to the UN. The UN's refusal to consider the matter precipitated widespread anti-British and anti-U.S. demonstrations in Cyprus and Greece. In 1955 the UN again decided not to take up the issue. Britain sought a political solution through direct talks with Greece and Turkey in London in 1955, but the negotiators failed to reach agreement. Athens rejected British offers of substantial autonomy for Cyprus and instead pressed demands for self-determination for the islanders.

The tripartite conference was followed by anti-Greek rioting in Turkey. In Nov. 1955 a new and more violent wave of terrorism swept Cyprus. British troops and installations came under repeated armed attacks by Greek Cypriots led by EOKA, the National Organization for the Cyprus Struggle, an extreme advocate of enosis. The outbreaks resulted in the imposition of a state of emergency Nov. 27, the shipment of British troop reinforcements to the island and their placement on a war footing.

Britain Proposes Constitutional Reforms

The first of a series of British proposals for constitutional reforms for Cyprus was submitted by Colonial Secy. Arthur Creech Jones Oct. 23, 1946. He announced that Cyprus Gov. Sir

Charles Woolley would invite all political elements on the island to form a Consultative Assembly to consider proposals for constitutional reforms, that a 10-year economic development plan had been drawn up and that the government would permit the return to Cyprus of persons who had been deported for participating in the 1931 disturbances.

The British plan was denounced Oct. 24 by the Cypriot press and the Ethnarchy Council, a body claiming to represent all Cypriot political parties. The council coupled its denunciation of London's proposal with the adoption of a resolution calling for *enosis.*

The council's proposal was formally submitted to the British government Feb. 7, 1948 at a meeting in London of Creech Jones with a Cypriot delegation headed by the bishop of Paphos, the ethnarch of Cyprus. The colonial secretary replied that Britain planned no change in the island's status.

In telegrams to British Prime Min. Clement Attlee and Creech Jones, representatives of the Turkish community in Cyprus had denied that the Ethnarchy Council spoke for all the people of the island; they said they favored the British plans for Cyprus.

Details of the reforms as advanced by Creech Jones May 12, 1948: (a) There would be a legislature of 22 elected members representing the island's residents (18 seats for the Greek community and 4 for the Turkish community) and 4 members representing British rule. (b) All male residents over 21 would be eligible to vote; suffrage would not be extended to women. (c) The legislature would be presided over by a chairman appointed by the governor; it would have no power to discuss the status of Cyprus within the British Commonwealth. The governor's consent would be required for the introduction of bills affecting finance, defense or foreign affairs.

In presenting the proposals, Creech Jones said that Cyprus' interests would "best be served by the adoption of a form of government which, without entailing any violent break in the administrative structure, will nevertheless provide for the active participation of the people of Cyprus in the conduct of their internal affairs."

The Consultative Assembly, which had been formed in accordance with the British proposal, met in Nicosia May 21 and approved the constitutional plan by 11-7 vote. 7 of the majority votes were cast by Turkish members and 4 by independent Greeks. The 7 minority votes were cast by leftwing Greek Cypriots, who then quit the assembly. The new Cyprus governor, Lord Winster, announced Aug. 12 the dissolution of the assembly in view of the leftwingers' action. Winster reiterated, however, that London's constitutional plan had not been withdrawn. He said Britain was prepared to take action "if at any time responsible and representative political leaders in Cyprus come forward to ask that those or comparable constitutional proposals be reexamined."

Winster's statement precipitated anti-British demonstrations throughout Cyprus. The outbreaks were organized by the Workers' Federation, and the demonstrators were told to prepare to fight for eventual union with Greece. Archbishop Makarios III, head of the Orthodox Church in Cyprus, who had urged Greek Cypriots to reject the British charter proposals, urged Britain May 14 to permit Cyprus to join Greece as an "act of justice" and "in fulfillment of the national demand." King Paul of Greece July 27 expressed backing for *enosis.*

Britain protested Paul's statement July 31, but Greek Premier Themistocles Sophoulis said the king had "merely repeated the national feelings already expressed in the Greek parliament."

Greek Cypriot Plebiscite Backs Enosis

Greek Cypriot support for *enosis* and an end to British rule was expressed in an islandwide plebiscite conducted Jan. 15-22, 1950 by the Ethnarchy Council. According to the results announced by the Council Jan. 29, 95.7% of an estimated total electorate of about 240,000 had cast ballots in favor of union with Greece. The Turkish Cypriot community did not participate in the vote.

Archbishop Makarios III Feb. 6 told Cyprus Gov. Sir Andrew Wright (who had replaced Gov. Winster May 9, 1949) that the outcome of the balloting justified the immediate union of Cyprus with Greece. Wright replied to Makarios Feb. 23 that Britain's position remained unchanged — the question of *enosis* was "closed." Wright had expressed similar views Dec. 17, 1949 in rejecting Makarios' request that the Cyprus government supervise the plebiscite. The projected balloting had been supported by all Greek Cypriot political parties, but the Turkish community denounced it. A resolution adopted by the Turkish Cypriots at a mass meeting in Dec. 1949 asserted that *enosis* would result in "economic ruin" for Cyprus. The statement urged continued British rule.

New British Constitutional Proposal

Britain announced July 28, 1954 that it was drawing up a new constitution, patterned after the constitutions of Britain's African and Asian colonies, that would grant Cyprus "a high degree of internal self-government." This charter would provide a legislature made up of an elected minority and a majority consisting of colonial officials and appointees. It was similar to the charter proposed by Britain in 1948.

Laborites criticized the move because it did not allow Cyprus to leave the British Commonwealth if its inhabitants wished.

Greek Foreign Min. Stephan Stephanopoulos said the proposal was an "improvement" over previous ones but unacceptable because it failed to grant Cyprus the right of self-determination.

Agitation for Enosis Increases

Britain's proposal of a new constitution not only failed to dampen the Greek Cypriot campaign for *enosis;* it actually spurred the drive to terminate British rule on the island.

5 days prior to the announcement of London's plan, Archbishop Makarios III said July 23, 1954 that the campaign for *enosis* would be peaceful, but he warned Britain that its military garrison in Cyprus was in a hostile atmosphere. Makarios, who

had visited Athens Feb. 5-Mar. 12, declared in Nicosia Mar. 12 that, at his meetings with King Paul and other Greek leaders, he had been assured that the Greek government would have raised the question of *enosis* at the UN if Britain had not agreed to bilateral negotiations with Greece before the General Assembly had its 9th annual session in September.

Alarmed by the growing agitation for union with Greece, British authorities on Cyprus Aug. 2 announced strict enforcement of the existing anti-sedition laws. Declaring that the campaign for *enosis* would no longer be tolerated, the government warned that the maximum penalties of 5 years' imprisonment would be imposed on persons found guilty of seditious conspiracies and publications aimed at advocating the alteration of the colony's status.

All 13 Greek-language newspapers in Cyprus suspended publication Aug. 3-9 in protest against the government's action. The editors Aug. 4 had sent a letter protesting to Prime Min. Sir Winston Churchill against the "restrictive measures against the press." The letter charged that the restrictions had been instituted "with the apparent aim of making ... the expression of popular feeling impossible at the time when the UN will be discussing a subject directly related to Cyprus."

The strict implementation of the anti-sedition laws was protested in a letter sent by Makarios Aug. 9 to the British Colonial Office in London. Makarios charged that the Cyprus government had "completely suppressed freedom of speech and the press." He vowed that Cypriots would continue their campaign for union with Greece by lawful means.

Demonstrations were staged throughout Greece Aug. 20 to back demands for *enosis*. Most shops and offices had been closed throughout Cyprus Aug. 12 in a 24-hour general strike for union with Greece and against the anti-sedition laws.

In defiance of the anti-sedition rulings, thousands of Cypriots converged on Nicosia Aug. 22 and heard Makarios declare in an address in the Phaneromeri Church: "We shall rise above the obstacles in our way, aiming at *enosis* and only at *enosis*." The British offer of a constitution was received with "indignation, and our protest is unanimous." "If our right is ignored by the United Nations, ... we shall regroup our forces and continue our struggle."

The Greek Cypriot drive for *enosis* was protested in a telegram sent to UN Secy. Gen. Dag Hammarskjold Aug. 22 by Dr. Fazil Kutchuk, secretary general of the Turkish National Party in Cyprus. Kutchuk declared: "100,000 Cyprus Turks strongly protest against the Greek government's position regarding the union of Cyprus with Greece and vehemently reject *enosis*, self-government or a plebiscite."

Greece Asks UN for Cyprus Plebiscite

Greece applied to the UN General Assembly Aug. 20, 1954 for a plebiscite to decide whether Cyprus would become part of Greece or continue under British rule. The request, signed by Greek Premier Alexander Papagos, was delivered to Secy. Gen. Hammarskjold by Christos X. Palamas, Greece's chief UN delegate.

Papagos said in his message that Britain's refusal to enter into direct negotiations with Greece on the status of Cyprus had aroused great indignation in his country which the Athens government could not ignore. London's position, Papagos stressed, jeopardized British-Greek relations, which were essential to the stability of the eastern Mediterranean. Greece's demand for UN intervention was necessary to achieve "a solution called for by justice, dignity and the sacred principles involved," Papagos said.

Sir Pierson Dixon, Britain's UN delegate, said that his government would oppose placing the Greek request on the Assembly agenda. He said Cyprus was "a territory in whose affairs the UN cannot intervene" since it was "entirely within the domestic jurisdiction" of Britain.

Assembly action on Greece's request for a plebiscite was blocked Dec. 15 when the Assembly's Political & Security Committee voted to postpone further consideration of the issue. Both Britain and Greece voted for a compromise resolution passed in committee Dec. 15. It said that "for the time being" it did "not seem appropriate" to take up the question of self-determination for Cyprus. This left the way open for Greece to submit the Cyprus question in 1955. The measure was passed by 49-0 (Soviet bloc, Burma, Chile, Ecuador, Indonesia, Thailand, Uruguay abstaining).

The committee had begun debate Dec. 14 on the Greek resolution calling on Britain to permit a plebiscite. The U.S., Turkey, Denmark, Sweden and Britain had immediately announced support of a New Zealand proposal to scrap the Greek resolution. The compromise was accepted later by Alexis Kyrou of Greece and Leslie Knox Munro of New Zealand.

Violence in Nicosia & Limassol, Riots in Greece

The refusal of the UN General Assembly to consider the Greek demand for *enosis* precipitated an outbreak of violence in Cyprus and anti-U.S. and anti-British demonstrations in Greece in Dec. 1954.

The most serious rioting to erupt in Cyprus for years occurred in Nicosia and Limassol Dec. 18-19 after nationalist and Communist organizations had called for a 24-hour general strike in protest against the UN's action. The strike call was generally effective, although municipal services were not interrupted. In Nicosia, demonstrators, made up largely of students, hurled stones at British-owned shops and autos and broke windows of the U.S. consulate. About 50 persons were arrested in clashes with the police.

The fighting in Limassol resulted in injuries to 23 persons, 2 of whom were wounded by British troops firing their weapons to disperse the mobs. Before order was restored, the demonstrators had hauled down the British flag and hoisted the Greek flag over the offices of the district commissioner. Several of the arrested demonstrators in Nicosia and Limassol were sentenced to 3 or 4 months' imprisonment.

The rioting prompted Cyprus government authorities to enact greater security measures, including a ban on meetings of more than 5 persons. This restriction, however, was lifted after a few days.

The rioting in Greece was centered in Athens, where about
50 students and 25 policemen were injured Dec. 14. The violence
occurred when several thousand students attempted to march on
the U.S. and British embassies. The marchers resorted to stones
and clubs when a police cordon blocked their way. The demonstrators denounced the U.S. as a "treacherous friend" for voting
against the plebiscite. Greek Premier Papagos declared Dec. 15
that Greece had been "betrayed" by its allies, including the U.S.,
on the Cyprus issue. But he apologized to U.S. Amb. Cavendish
Cannon for the anti-American riots in Athens.

London Talks Deadlock Spurs Anti-Greek Riots

Foreign Mins. Harold Macmillan of Britain, Fatin Rustu
Zorlu of Turkey and Stephan Stephanopoulos of Greece conferred in London Aug. 29-Sept. 7, 1955 on the future of Cyprus.
The talks were officially "suspended" after Greece and Turkey
rejected a British proposal for self-government for the colony.
Objections were based on diametrically opposite reasons. Greece
favored self-government if it would lead to self-determination by
Cyprus, where the Greek majority would be expected to favor
union with Greece. Turkey was satisfied with British sovereignty
over the island.

Macmillan said self-determination "could not be applied
under conditions that rule in the Mediterranean." He said: "We
do not accept the principle of self-determination as one of universal application. We think that exceptions must be made in view of
geographical, traditional, historical, strategic and other con-
siderations."

Macmillan reiterated Britain's offer to Cyprus of a new
constitution and an assembly that would have the majority of its
members elected by the Cypriots. Government functions would
be gradually transferred to Cypriot ministers responsible to the
assembly. A Cypriot chief minister would be elected eventually,
but Britain would retain sovereignty. Macmillan also suggested
that a permanent British-Greek-Turkish commission supervise
implementation of the self-rule process. During the talks,
Macmillan invited Greece and Turkey to join Britain in making
greater use of Cyprus for the mutual defense of the 3 countries.

Britain had initiated the London conference. Prime Min. Anthony Eden had disclosed June 29 that his government had extended invitations to Greece and Turkey to attend the talks.

Opposition to the tripartite conference had been expressed by Archbishop Makarios before it opened. In a statement issued July 16, following 6 days of talks with Greek officials in Athens, Makarios declared that the London parley was "a trap aimed at torpedoing recourse" to the UN and that "the people of Cyprus will never accept any decisions of the London conference which do not accord with their rights and aspirations, even if those decisions are endorsed by the Greek government." Makarios said he would have preferred to make an immediate appeal to the UN rather than to submit the Cyprus question to the 3 powers.

The failure of the London talks coincided with demonstrations in Greece and Turkey. A dynamite explosion Sept. 6 in the garden of the Turkish consulate in Salonika, in northern Greece, touched off Turkish riots against Greek shops in Istanbul and Izmir (Smyrna) the same day. The demonstrations followed reports in the Turkish cities that the Salonika dynamiting had damaged the birthplace of Kemal Atatürk, first president of the Turkish Republic. Martial law was imposed in Istanbul, Izmir and Ankara. Greece protested to Turkey Sept. 7 against the demonstrations.

NATO's Permanent Council (of ambassadors) met in Paris Sept. 8 for a discussion of the anti-Greek demonstrations. Turkey expressed regret over the disturbances and assured the council that measures had been taken to prevent a recurrence. Greece implied that the outbreaks had been tolerated by Turkish officials. The council accepted Turkey's assurances.

The Turkish state radio Sept. 10 announced the resignation of Interior Min. Namig Gedik and the transfer of 2 other top internal security officials. No reason was given for the changes. The Turkish Defense Ministry Sept. 9 relieved 3 generals who had held key posts in Istanbul at the time of the Sept. 6 disorders. The ministry said their removal followed a full investigation of the disturbances. At least 3,000 persons were reported arrested in Istanbul on charges of looting and violence. Turkey expressed "deep regret" to the Greek government Sept. 12 and promised compensation for damaged property, estimated unofficially at $300 million.

Greek Premier Constantine Karamanlis announced Oct. 11 that Greek forces would not take part in NATO exercises until issues left by the anti-Greek riots in Turkey were settled.

UN Again Bars Cyprus Issue

The UN General Assembly's Steering Committee Sept. 21, 1955 rejected a Greek proposal to place discussion of the Cyprus issue on the Assembly's agenda. The U.S., which had abstained in a similar vote in 1954, joined Britain, France, Chile, Luxembourg, New Zealand and Norway in voting against the Greek proposal, which was supported by the USSR, Poland, Egypt and Mexico. Nationalist China, Ethiopia, Haiti and Thailand abstained.

British State Min. Anthony Nutting told the committee that Cyprus was "indisputably a British responsibility" and therefore outside UN jurisdiction. He said Greece was urging Cypriots to resort to violence, but "my government devoutly hopes that the door of friendly consultation will not remain closed for long."

U.S. Amb.-to-UN Henry Cabot Lodge, explaining the change in the U.S. position, said that in 1954 the U.S. was "dubious" about bringing the Cyprus issue before the Assembly because it doubted that "positive results could be achieved here." He said the debate then "was conducted in a spirit of relative moderation," but "since then, the situation has become more inflamed." Lodge added that this was one occasion "when quiet diplomacy is far more effective than public debate."

The General Assembly Sept. 23 upheld its Steering Committee's decision to shelve discussion of the Cyprus issue. The Assembly vote: 28-22, with 10 abstentions.

Emergency Rule Follows Increased Unrest

Field Marshal Sir John Harding, governor of Cyprus (appointed Sept. 25, 1955), proclaimed a state of emergency in Cyprus Nov. 26, 1955 after months of disorders were climaxed by the deaths of 5 British soldiers in a single week in *enosis* demonstrations. The emergency proclamation authorized the death penalty for carrying arms or ammunition without authority, life imprisonment for sabotage against public utilities or communications.

The 10,000-man British force on the island was placed on a war footing Nov. 28 for a period of 3 months as a parallel measure to the proclamation of the state of emergency.

Archbishop Makarios said Nov. 27 that the emergency decree was a British attempt to "bend the national resistance of the people" by force. In a sermon Nov. 30, he called the emergency measures "completely totalitarian and Hitlerian."

Talks between Harding and Makarios broke down Oct. 11, when Harding said in a radio speech that he had asked the archbishop to support his proposals to end violence in Cyprus so that steps could be taken toward Cypriot self-government.

The sharp attacks, aimed largely at British installations and troops, had erupted in June and were spearheaded by EOKA, the National Organization for the Cyprus Struggle. The organization had proclaimed a terrorist campaign to back demands for merger of Cyprus with Greece.

The Cyprus government Sept. 15 issued an order banning EOKA for one year because it had promoted "disorder and the spread of sedition." In a further crackdown against the spreading violence, the government decreed that accused terrorists would no longer appear before a magistrate for preliminary hearing but would be held for court trial.

A secret Turkish Cypriot organization calling itself Volkan had circulated leaflets Sept. 9 threatening reprisals against EOKA if any attacks were directed against Turkish officials, policemen or civilians in Cyprus. Volkan charged that EOKA had included the names of prominent Turkish Cypriots on a "terror list."

Britain Compromises on Self-Determination

British Foreign Secy. Harold Macmillan told Commons Dec. 5, 1955 that Britain's stand against self-determination for Cyprus "within the foreseeable future" had changed to allow consideration of self-determination "some time and in certain conditions." Macmillan urged Greek, Turkish and Cypriot cooperation to help end Communist-inspired "terrorism" on Cyprus. Britain outlawed the 20,000-member Communist Party on Cyprus Dec. 14 and arrested 135 leading members.

Archbishop Makarios disclosed Dec. 7 that he had rejected the latest British offer because it was "made dependent" on "certain prerequisites that rendered self-determination unattainable."

APPROACH TO SELF-RULE 1956-8

Britain renewed efforts to find a solution to the constitutional crisis as talks were held in Feb. 1956 with Archbishop Makarios and Turkish Cypriot leaders. The negotiations with Makarios foundered largely on the archbishop's insistence on guarantees of a Greek Cypriot majority in a proposed parliament. The breakdown in the talks was followed by the deportation of Makarios and 3 other Greek Orthodox churchmen to the Seychelle Islands Mar. 9. They were charged with supporting and fomenting anti-British terrorism Makarios was released from detention Mar. 28, 1957 but was not permitted to return to Cyprus. He went to Greece instead.

Makarios' ouster from Cyprus precipitated a widespread terror campaign launched by pro-enosis EOKA forces against British troops on the island. The violence mounted in intensity as Turkish Cypriots entered the fighting and attacked Greek Cypriot villages. Casualties were high among all 3 parties to the conflict. The violence was halted by an EOKA truce in Aug. 1956, but the Greek Cypriot terrorists resumed their assaults Aug. 30, and sporadic clashes continued through September.

Britain offered a new constitutional proposal in Aug. 1957, but the Greek Cypriots rejected it and insisted on self-determination. Greece carried the fight for self-rule to the UN, but the world body rebuffed Athens' proposals that it intervene.

Violence erupted again in 1957-8 with Turkish Cypriots taking an increasing role in the fighting. They brought to the communal struggle a new political demand — the partition of Cyprus into Greek and Turkish zones. The bloodshed involving the 2 communities caused strained relations between Greece and Turkey. The fighting in 1958 led Greece June 15 to sever all military links with Turkey under NATO's Southeast European Command.

Britain embarked on a bolder step to bring peace to the island by proposing June 19, 1958 a plan in which the Greek and Turkish Cypriots would be granted self-government in partnership while Britain retained sovereignty over the island. A modified version of the plan went into effect Oct. 1. The Turkish Cypriots approved, but the Greek Cypriots denounced the arrangement as a scheme to perpetuate British rule of Cyprus.

British Talks with Makarios Fail

British Colonial Secy. Alan Lennox-Boyd met in Cyprus Feb. 26-29, 1956 with Archbishop Makarios and Gov. Sir John Harding to discuss the constitutional future of the island. He also conferred with Fazil Kutchuk and other Turkish Cypriot leaders. In a report to the British House of Commons Mar. 5, Lennox-Boyd said the negotiations with Makarios had broken down on 3 basic issues: (1) Amnesty terms for Cypriot terrorists in British jails. (221 Cypriots were under arrest, and 4 of them were under death sentence.) (2) British insistence that the British governor general maintain control of internal security as long as necessary. (3) The archbishop's insistence that the elected majority of the proposed Cypriot parliament be defined in the constitution to make certain it would be Greek.

Lennox-Boyd told Commons that he had offered concessions on the 3 points during his final talk with Makarios Feb. 29, but, he said, Makarios declined to cooperate, and, even if agreement had been reached, "a new series of demands which had not yet emerged would have raised their heads." Lennox-Boyd said Makarios had "upped his price" at each stage of the 5-month negotiations with Harding. Lennox-Boyd said that, when he himself arrived in Cyprus, "general agreement had been reached on the need to establish self-government, and the principle of self-determination was no longer a stumbling block."

British Exile Makarios to Seychelles

Archbishop Makarios and 3 other high-ranking Greek Orthodox churchmen were deported from Cyprus to the Seychelle Islands in the Indian Ocean by British authorities Mar. 9, 1956 as active supporters of anti-British terrorism. The colonial government in Nicosia, in explaining Makarios' deportation by order of Gov. Harding, said Mar. 9 that Britain had continued negotiations with Makarios the past 5 months despite accumulating evidence that the archbishop was "personally implicated in the terrorist activities" of EOKA. Negotiations failed, the statement said, because of Makarios' "refusal to abandon the weapons of violence and intimidation in the pursuit of his political ends." Matters still in dispute between Britain and pro-Greek Cypriots "cannot possibly ... justify or excuse the continued resort to the violence and extreme methods which are still rife on the island," and Makarios' removal was necessary to "promoting peace, order and good government," the statement concluded.

Makarios was arrested while boarding an Athens-bound airliner in Nicosia Mar. 9. (Welcoming delegations were waiting for him at the Athens airport when his arrest was announced.) British authorities on Cyprus simultaneously arrested: Bishop Kyprianos of Kyrenia, 48, 4th-ranking Cypriot Orthodox churchman; Polykarpos Ioannides, the bishop of Kyrenia's secretary; Papastayros Papa-Agathangelou, a priest and assistant to Makarios. The 4 were flown to Mombasa, Kenya and put aboard a British frigate for transfer to Mahe Island, one of the Seychelles group in the Indian Ocean 950 miles off the Kenya coast. The British did not disclose where they were being sent until they were aboard the frigate and it had sailed for the Seychelles Mar. 10. The events leading to Makarios' ouster were described in a memo issued by British authorities in Nicosia Mar. 9. *The document said:*

"Today the governor, Field Marshal Sir John Harding, ordered the deportation of Archbishop Makarios under Regulation VII of the Emergency Powers (Public Safety & Order) Regulations. The archbishop has already left the island under escort for a destination which will be announced later.

"The governor entered into discussions on the political and constitutional future of the island with Archbishop Makarios as being the traditional leader of the Greek Cypriot community. In embarking on these discussions the governor was aware that there were grounds for believing that the archbishop was per-

sonally implicated in the terrorism. Nevertheless, the governor decided to negotiate with him in the hope that he might be induced to denounce violence and to
advise his fellow-countrymen to follow his lead. . . .

"Over the past 5 months, while the discussions have proceeded, further evidence, both direct and circumstantial, has accumulated to show the extent to
which the archbishop has been personally implicated in EOKA's activities. Nevertheless, the governor has pursued these discussions to the furthest possible limit of
conciliation and concession in the hope that the archbishop might be induced to
denounce violence and so to open the door to cooperation and orderly constitutional progress.

"This hope has now been disappointed by the archbishop's refusal to abandon
the weapons of violence and intimidation in the pursuit of his political aims. The
matters over which he has broken off the discussions cannot possibly be held to
justify or excuse the continued resort to violent and extreme methods which are
still rife in the island, and which have recently culminated in a dastardly attempt
to wreck an aircraft carrying British servicemen and their families. It is impossible to escape the conclusion that the archbishop is now so far committed to the
use of violence for political ends that he either cannot or will not abandon it.

"The governor has therefore reluctantly concluded that the archbishop now
personally constitutes a major obstacle to a return to peaceful conditions and that
his influence must therefore be removed from the island in the interest of promoting peace, order, and good government."

The direct reasons for Gov. Harding's decisions to deport Makarios were made public in this explanatory statement:

"(1) The governor reached his decision to order the archbishop's deportation
in the light not only of his overt seditious activities but also of a large volume of
evidence indicating that the archbishop has himself been deeply implicated in the
campaign of terrorism launched by the organization known as EOKA.

"In recent months, as the security forces have penetrated further into the
terrorist organization, evidence of the archbishop's complicity has accumulated
from many different sources. The governor has scrutinized the information thus
collected with the greatest possible care and has reluctantly reached the conclusion that it establishes beyond all reasonable doubt that the archbishop has not
merely countenanced but has actively fostered terrorism in order to promote his
political aims. While overtly and in apparent good faith conducting negotiations
for a political settlement of the island's future, the archbishop has surreptitiously
encouraged and abetted the terrorists in order to improve his own bargaining
position in the negotiations.

"(2) The archbishop's association with the elements out of which EOKA has
emerged dates back to 1951, when, soon after his election as archbishop, he
personally undertook the formation of the extreme nationalist youth organization
known as 'Peon.'

"(3) When establishing branches of that organization, the archbishop said
that it would be modelled on the lines of the National Youth Organization established under the Metaxas regime in Greece. He spoke of the need for secrecy and

sacrifices, for the boycott of British goods and the British way of life, for the destruction of shops displaying English signs, for the production of a clandestine newspaper and for establishment of contributory funds for the national struggle. In July 1951 Col. Grivas (now reported to be the leader of EOKA) arrived in Cyprus at the archbishop's invitation to advise on the organization of 'Peon,' which was to follow that of Grivas' extremist organization in Greece.

"(4) During the period 1951-3 evidence accumulated that this organization, to which the archbishop continued to give his personal patronage, was being used for subversive purposes and was preparing for a resort to violence. It developed contacts with irredentist agencies in Greece. Its members were involved in the dissemination of subversive propaganda and in illegal demonstrations resulting in damage to property. In June 1953 the organization was rendered illegal by the withdrawal of its registration under the Clubs Law.

"(5) It continued to function underground and provided the organizational basis and staff on which EOKA was later built. Its ex-general secretary (Stavros Poskotis) and several persons who had been leading members were among a group of terrorists who perpetrated the first EOKA outrages at Larnaca on Apr. 1, 1955. They were sentenced to terms of imprisonment ranging from 3 to 9 years.

"Another person (Evghenios Cotsapas) who, as district secretary, had taken a leading part in establishing the branch at Limassol, was caught red-handed on Nov. 18, 1955, carrying bombs in his car and was sentenced to 3 years' imprisonment. He is the son of an Ethnarchy councillor who is himself now in detention.

"No fewer than 3 out of the 5 members of the former Nicosia district committee of the organization (Christor Eleftherion Evangelos Evangelakis and Markos Dvakos) are now members of the terrorist gangs at large in the island, and one of these was a personal protege of the archbishop. Such were the men to whom Archbishop Makarios entrusted the formation of a youth organization under his personal patronage.

"(6) In Aug. 1954, a certain Zephirios Valvis visited Cyprus at the archbishop's request. This man is a Greek national, and by profession a lawyer practising at Athens. He is now known to have been one of the principal lieutenants of Col. Grivas and a member of an organization in Greece which has been responsible for arranging shipments of arms and explosives to the terrorists in Cyprus. He had a number of meetings with the archbishop and attended a meeting of the Holy Synod and of other leading enosists held at Mesapotamos monastery and presided over by the archbishop. There is reason to believe that at that meeting the plans were laid which later bore fruit in the organized violence and terrorism of EOKA.

"(7) Over the past 2 years information has been received from a number of different sources indicating that the archbishop has personally supplied funds to agents in Greece for the purchase and supply of arms and explosives for terrorist operations in Cyprus. In particular, it is reported that a large sum from the monies which the archbishop collected from Greek communities in the United States during his visit there in 1954 was handed over by him in Athens to Valvis for the purchase and delivery of explosives, which were later seized while being smuggled into Cyprus in the Greek schooner *Aghios Gheorghios*.

"The governor has carefully examined these various reports and is satisfied that they establish beyond doubt that the archbishop has provided large sums of money to irredentist agencies in Greece and, in so doing, was aware that they would be used for the shipment of arms and explosives to Cyprus.

"(8) Funds under the archbishop's control are known to have been used to pay fines imposed by the courts on persons who had taken part in illegal political activities in Cyprus. Members of the Greek Orthodox community requiring the services of the archbishopric have been required to contribute to a fund for the 'national struggle,' and the various fees and dues charged for such services have been increased with the same object.

"(9) The archbishopric has been used for the production of EOKA leaflets on a scale which would have been impossible without the archbishop's connivance.

"(10) The archbishopric has also been used for the temporary storage of arms and grenades.

"(11) There is strong circumstantial evidence to show that the timing and intensity of terrorist activities have been adjusted to strengthen the bargaining position of the archbishop during the course of his negotiations with the governor. It is also noticeable that, during his absences from the island in April-May and October-November of last year, a marked lull occurred in terrorist activity.

"(12) Besides his contacts with Grivas and his lieutenant, Valvis, the archbishop's personal relations with known members of the EOKA organization are such as to provide strong corroboration of his complicity in the activities of the terrorists. The organizer of the *Aghios Gheorghios* gun-running venture was Socrates Loizides, brother of the ethnarchy councillor, Savvas Loizides, who has frequently acted as the archbishop's spokesman in Athens.

"Certain of the detailed arrangements for this shipment were made by Andreas Azinas, a personal protege of the archbishop who had previously been elected secretary general of the Pan-Cyprian Farmers' Union with support from the archbishop. This man is now wanted by the police for his part in the *Aghios Gheorghios* case.

"The convicted terrorist Stavros Poskotis, whom the archbishop selected as secretary general of the youth organization 'Peon,' was employed in the printing works belonging to the archbishopric. It was there, too, that the archbishop's close kinsman Charalambos Mouskos was employed before he embarked on the career of murder and violence which terminated in his being shot dead in a gun battle with a member of the security forces. It was on the archbishop's orders that this man was given shelter and medical treatment in the Kykko monastery.

"When Karaolis, the convicted murderer of a police constable, was arrested, it was another employe of the archbishopric printing works who was taking him in his car to join the terrorist gang then operating in the Kyrenia hills. The driver of the car absconded and is still wanted by the police.

"(13) Finally, one of the most significant and surely one of the most culpable aspects of the archbishop's conduct is his persistent failure, despite his position as the religious leader of the Greek Cypriot Orthodox Christian community, to condemn the wickedness and brutality of EOKA's methods. At once, on the outbreak of terrorism last April, he was urged by the then governor to denounce violence. He failed to do so. He failed even to comment on the patently irreligious oath which the terrorists were urging schoolchildren to take. Further attempts to induce him to give his community a lead against terrorism were also fruitless.

"He has remained silent while policemen and soldiers have been murdered in cold blood, while women and children have been killed and maimed by bombs, while a Cypriot woman was shot and wounded for the 2d time as she lay in hospital recovering from a previous terrorist attack, and even while he stood by the coffin of an abbot of his own church who was brutally murdered by terrorists in his own monastery. His silence has understandably been accepted among his community as not merely condoning, but even approving, assassination and bomb-throwing. He has confirmed that interpretation by referring in sermons to convicted terrorists as patriots and by urging his fellow-countrymen to take the law into their own hands.

"And now, in the last few weeks, he has sought positively to exploit his power to influence the members of his church against violence by seeking to bargain this against concessions from H.M. Government on the form of a constitution and on the grant of an amnesty to terrorists convicted of crimes of violence.

"(14) On this evidence the governor has decided that the example and influence of Archbishop Makarios is so detrimental to public safety and public order that his continued presence in the island can no longer be tolerated. He has taken this step only after the most careful and deliberate consideration. He is well aware of the pain and dismay that this measure will cause not only among the Greek Orthodox community in Cyprus but in the world at large.

"(15) So long as there were grounds to hope that the archbishop might be induced to use the influence which he possesses among his community to lead them away from violence, disorder and fear and back to the path of peace and democratic rule, the governor was of the opinion that the good of the people of Cyprus as a whole compelled him to overlook the shameful record of the archbishop's complicity in bloodshed, intimidation and the tyrannous suppression of free opinion.

"The archbishop has chosen to reject the offer of a new and constructive approach to the island's political problems and to continue to seek to gain his ends by force. With that he has finally removed any compunction that the governor may have felt against dealing with him, not as a responsible political leader, and still less as the head of a Christian church, but in that character which he has himself chosen to prefer — the leader of a political campaign which relies on the use of ruthless violence and terrorism."

50,000 British troops and policemen, acting under emergency powers regulations, intensified their anti-terrorist patrols of the island as soon as Makarios' deportation was announced Mar. 9. Many persons in Nicosia and other towns were halted in the streets and searched for hidden weapons.

Streets in Nicosia were almost deserted Mar. 10 as residents stayed indoors. Terrorist attacks continued Mar. 9-10 as bombs were hurled at British patrols in Famagusta and Kathikas and at a British house in Limassol, and guerrillas tried unsuccessfully to ambush a British patrol near Paphos. Other demonstrations occurred in Polis and Pakhna. The village of Pakhna was fined $16,800 for damage to a police station and its furniture and records caused by rioters.

Gov. Harding's office Mar. 10 banned press and radio distribution of news reports "likely to cause alarm or despondency or be prejudicial to" public safety and order.

Greek Cypriots staged a one-day general strike Mar. 10 in protest against Makarios' exile.

In debate in the British House of Commons Mar. 14, British Prime Min. Sir Anthony Eden defended his policies on Cyprus and the deportation of Makarios. Eden won a 317-251 vote of confidence after the defeat of a Labor Party motion of censure. Eden told Commons that British commitments to allies and interests in the Middle East required "the sure and unfettered use of Cyprus" as a British base. "The welfare and lives of our people depend on Cyprus as a protective guard and staging post to take care of their interests — above all, oil," Eden said. "This is not imperialism. It should be the plain duty of any government, and we intend to discharge it." Eden said that the failure of talks with Makarios and his subsequent exile came after discussions in which "all we asked for was a declaration against the use of violence and we did not get it."

The Greek government recalled Amb. Basil Mostra from London Mar. 9 in protest against the banishment of Makarios from Cyprus. Riots against the British action were staged Mar. 10 in Athens and Salonika. Greek demonstrators ransacked the British consulate in Candia, Crete Mar. 10, burning the British flag and forcing the consul and his staff to flee to a secret refuge under police protection.

The Holy Synod of the Greek Orthodox Church in Athens denounced Makarios' banishment Mar. 10 as "a nefarious act reminiscent of the dark days of serfdom." The protest statement was sent to prelates of other Orthodox churches, including Patriarch Alexius of Moscow, to the Churches of England, Sweden and Norway and to the World Federation of Churches.

The teaching of English in Greek elementary and high schools was suspended indefinitely Mar. 11 in protest against Makarios' exile. However, the Greek government canceled nationwide demonstrations of "grief and anger" in support of Makarios that it had planned for Mar. 12. Premier Constantine Karamanlis' office explained that "anti-national" [Communist] elements had planned to exploit the demonstrations. Greek troops had been assigned to defend the U.S., British and Turkish embassies in Athens against possible attack by rioters.

Archbishop Spyridon of Athens & All Greece, head of the Greek Orthodox Church and chairman of the Pan-Hellenic Committee for Union with Cyprus, broadcast his indorsement of the government's cancellation of the demonstrations and promised to do "everything in my power for the liberation of" Makarios. The Cyprus ethnarchy of the Orthodox church warned Mar. 19 that Makarios' exile had "destroyed, or at least postponed until his return, the only existing chance for a peaceful settlement of the Cyprus question."

U.S. Asst. State Secy. Livingston T. Merchant, in a discussion of the dispute over Cyprus Mar. 12 with British Amb.-to-U.S. Sir Roger Makins, was reported to have urged that the British make an effort to reestablish negotiations with Cypriot leaders. But Colonial Secy. Alan Lennox-Boyd told the House of Commons Mar. 12 he doubted that talks could be revived until moderate Cypriots' "freedom to think and speak for themselves has been, through the restoration of order, restored to the people of Cyprus... who would hesitate to come forward as leaders when they would be branded as traitors" by EOKA extremists.

A statement of the U.S.' "sympathetic concern... over recent developments in Cyprus" was delivered to the Greek government Mar. 13 by U.S. Amb.-to-Greece Cavendish W. Cannon, who assured Greece of the U.S.' "continued interest... in the establishment of a government truly representative of the people of Cyprus." Cannon also conveyed to Greek Foreign Min. Spyros Theotokis assurance that the U.S. had not known in advance of the British plan to deport Makarios.

Cannon's expression of "sympathetic concern" to Greece was criticized by several leading British newspapers Mar. 13, and London directed Amb. Makins to ask the U.S. State Department for an explanation. The State Department then issued a statement disavowing partiality on the British-Greek dispute and expressing readiness "to assist our friends" in finding a "fair and just solution." British State Min. Sir Anthony Nutting told U.S. Amb.-to-Britain Winthrop W. Aldrich Mar. 14 of the British government's displeasure at Cannon's remarks.

Critical American comments on Britain's Cyprus policies were referred to by Prime Min. Eden Mar. 14 when he said of a statement by Greek Premier Constantine Karamanlis that the U.S. had saved Greece from communism: "It was the British government and British forces which [in 1944-5]... delivered Greece... at the cost of British dead and wounded from... the certainty of Communist rule."

Terrorism & Armed Clashes

Greek Cypriot armed attacks on British forces in Cyprus intensified during March-June 1956. Heavy casualties, including many fatalities, were inflicted by both sides. The violence took a turn for the worse as Greek and Turkish Cypriots began to engage in serious clashes with each other.

At the outset of the latest phase of violence, Gov. Harding warned Mar. 18 that Britain would not reopen negotiations on Cypriot self-rule or the return of exiled Archbishop Makarios until after terrorism had been crushed. He said that "long and patient negotiations" with Makarios had convinced him the archbishop would accept nothing but "virtual control of the island [and]... as evidence accumulated, it became clear to me that the archbishop was so deeply committed to cooperation with the EOKA that he could not condemn violence."

Anti-British terrorism and unrest Mar. 14-19 was marked by the killing of 2 Britons and 6 Cypriots and the wounding of 10 other Britons and 19 Cypriots. Additional injuries resulted from clashes Mar. 19-20 between Greek and Turkish Cypriots. *Among events reported:*

March incidents — A British police sergeant was killed by terrorist gunfire in Nicosia Mar. 14 while he patrolled with a Turkish Cypriot policeman, who was wounded. British forces sealed off the center of the city in an attempt to find the assassin. After 400 families ignored an appeal for information on the slaying, the British expelled 10 families from their homes and closed 18 shops in the area.

A 7-year-old Cypriot boy was killed in Larnaca Mar. 14 when a British soldier fired one shot into a Cypriot mob that had stoned 2 Army trucks. 2 Cypriots were shot to death Mar. 14 in a coffee house in Dhora by 3 masked men.

In Nicosia Mar.15 the wife and child of a British soldier were injured when a bomb was thrown into their home; a British soldier was wounded near Army headquarters; 2 cyclists (one captured later) fired on, but missed, 2 British security policemen.

In the most severe attack on British forces during the past year of terrorist incidents, a band of suspected EOKA men ambushed a motorized patrol Mar. 17 near Khandria and wounded 5 British commandos. One terrorist, identified as a local farmer, was killed. Khandria and 6 other mountain towns in the ambush area were placed under 24-hour curfew.

The bombing of a British Army truck Mar 17 in Lapithos resulted in the death of one soldier, injuries to 2 others. British authorities fined the village £700 ($19,600) for the incident and for earlier disorders.

A Cypriot, believed to have been suspected of collaboration with the British, was shot to death Mar. 18 in a Kythrea church by 4 masked men.

Near Limassol Mar. 18, a Turkish Cypriot was killed and another wounded when they reportedly behaved threateningly while British troops conducted a search for hidden weapons.

17 Cypriots were injured Mar. 19 in riots in Vasilia, where Greek Cypriot townsmen returned from a religious festival and attacked the village's Turkish quarter, stoned its residents and attempted to set fire to several houses. British forces broke up the riot, the first major outbreak between the 2 Cypriot ethnic groups in several years. Vasilias was placed under curfew.

Turkish Cypriots retaliated for the Vasilia incident by stoning Greek Cypriot stores in Nicosia Mar. 20 until Turkish Cypriot leader Fazil Kutchuk persuaded them to end the demonstration. Kutchuk said at a rally in the Turkish quarter of Nicosia that Turkey would occupy Cyprus if the British left. He told foreign newsmen in Nicosia Mar. 20 that he would protest to the UN, Britain and Turkey against Greek Cypriots' "barbarity" in Vasilia but was trying not to inflame Turkish Cypriots and was seeking to prevent "a terrible civil war" from breaking out on the island immediately.

British authorities enforced a 24-hour curfew in 13 major towns and cities Mar. 25-26 during the 135th anniversary of Greek national independence from Turkish rule (Mar. 25). The curfew held an estimated 300,000 persons indoors and banned the holiday's usual church services, parades and pro-Greek speeches. British officials said they believed "terrorist groups" had planned to exploit the traditional celebrations to further the *enosis* (union-with-Greece) campaign. Bishop Anthimos of Kitium, acting Cypriot Orthodox Church leader, had urged mass attendance at special services and prayers for the return of exiled Archbishop Makarios. Anthimos had arrived in Nicosia Mar. 12 to take over Makarios' duties during his exile.

600 persons reported arrested for minor curfew infringements were freed under bail Mar. 26. A Cypriot general strike, rumored to be planned for Mar. 26, failed to materialize. (52 Greek Cypriot shopkeepers in Nicosia had been charged Mar. 22 with having staged an "illegal strike" by closing Mar. 14 in protest against Makarios' exile.)

Gov. Harding removed all Cypriot members of his Government House staff Mar. 22 after the discovery Mar. 20 of a time bomb in his bedroom. Neophitos Sophocleos, Harding's servant, who had disappeared Mar. 21, was suspected of having placed the bomb. It was removed from Harding's room and defused.

A British Army corporal was killed and 2 other soldiers wounded Mar. 21 in Famagusta when a terrorist bomb was thrown into their truck. A former Greek Cypriot policeman was killed Mar. 22 by a gunman near the village of Xeros. A bomb thrown at a British patrol in the port of Paphos Mar. 22 injured a Greek Cypriot woman, and a car belonging to a U.S. citizen working with the U.S. consulate in Kyrenia was set afire.

2 members of a British security patrol were killed Mar. 27 in Phrenaros, near Famagusta, by automatic weapons fire from ambush. A Cypriot customs official was killed by terrorist gunfire Mar. 27 in Limassol, reportedly as part of an EOKA activist campaign to pressure customs staffs into passing arms shipments from abroad. Bomb explosions were reported Mar. 27 in Limassol, where 3 suspects were arrested; Lefka, where a military vehicle was damaged and a Cypriot boy, 13, wounded when soldiers fired on suspects nearby; Famagusta, where a bomb was thrown into the yard of a security force member's home.

A British officer and an enlisted man were killed Mar. 28 when Cypriot terrorists ambushed a security patrol in Phrenaros. The British arrested 16 villagers and placed the town under a curfew, but the British Mar. 29 revoked a £1,500 fine, reportedly after information was given on the attack. 21 suspected EOKA adherents were held Mar. 28 in Limassol. 4 bombing incidents were reported there and in Larnaca Mar. 31. 29 persons were arrested Mar. 31 in searches of suspected terrorist hideouts, including a monastery near Nicosia.

Bishop Anthimos told 4,000 worshipers in Nicosia Mar. 31 that Cypriots "will fight the British with every means at our disposal." Leaflets distributed in the church said EOKA would "continue to fight until one day the British will salute the Greek flag flying over Cyprus."

A curfew was imposed on Nicosia Mar. 31-Apr. 2 to prevent outbreaks on the first anniversary of the initial EOKA attack there Apr. 1, 1955.

Charges of maltreatment of Cypriot prisoners were lodged against the British Mar. 31 by Andreas Bouyouras, mayor of Famagusta, where a Greek Cypriot policeman was wounded the same day by terrorists.

April incidents — The first killing of a British civilian in Cyprus during the terrorist campaign was reported Apr. 1 in Limassol, where a Cypriot girl, 12, was fatally injured by a bomb Apr. 2. British authorities Apr. 1 reported these casualty and arrest totals for the past year: 24 British soldiers, 8 policemen, 24 Greek civilians and 12 terrorists killed; 114 soldiers and policemen, 30 Greek and Cypriot policemen, 61 civilians and 20 terrorists wounded; 35 terrorists captured.

Rioting high school students in Paphos, reportedly accompanied by 2 Ortho-dox priests, threw stones and bombs at British policemen and troops Apr. 2 after the British broke up their attempt to parade under the Greek flag. 2 schools in Paphos were closed after the incident. British officials said Apr. 2 that 37 of 57 secondary schools on Cyprus had been closed, 31 by action of the Cypriots.

Terrorist incidents Apr. 11-23 resulted in the killings of 4 members of the British security forces, 8 Greek Cypriots and 2 Turkish Cypriots. The deaths of the 2 Turkish Cypriots Apr. 23 were followed by riots Apr. 24 in which Turkish Cypriots raided Greek shops in Nicosia. A terrorist bomb Apr. 27 destroyed a plane of the British-owned Cyprus Airways at Nicosia Airport.

Greek Cypriot rebels executed — British military authorities hanged 2 Greek Cypriots — Michael Savva Karaolis, 22, and Andreas Demetriou, 23 — in Nicosia May 10 after Gov. Harding May 8 had refused appeals for clemency from Cypriot religious leaders. The British Labor Party and U.S. State Secy. John Foster Dulles reportedly had urged stays of execution to prevent further Cypriot unrest. Karaolis, first Cypriot rebel to be sentenced to death in 78 years of British rule on Cyprus, had been convicted Apr. 14 of killing a Greek Cypriot policeman in Aug. 1955. Demetriou was convicted and sentenced to death for wounding a British businessman in Nov. 1955. (3 persons were killed and 124 injured May 9 when Greek crowds protesting the impending executions clashed with police and attempted to storm the British consulate in Salonika and U.S. Information Agency Office in Athens. Cyprus, under heavy British curfew and general strike, was reported calm before the hangings, but terrorists in Ktima May 9 killed a British officer and wounded 2 soldiers and 4 Greek Cypriots.)

Other May incidents — Terrorist leaflets scattered in Nicosia May 11 claimed that EOKA activists had hanged 2 British Army corporals in reprisal for the 2 Cypriot executions. The leaflets, signed by "the Leader Dighenis [pseudo-nym of George Grivas]," said that EOKA would "answer hanging with hanging and torture with torture" and that the bodies of the 2 men would not be returned "following the example of the occupation forces toward the murdered Greek patriots." A 19-year-old Cypriot distributing the leaflets was killed when he ran from British troops in Nicosia May 11.

EOKA leaflets May 15 called for "all honest leftists" in the Cypriot Com-munist Party (AKEL) to join the battle for independence. The leaflets again were signed "Dighenis." British military authorities May 3 had posted a £10,000 ($28,000) reward and offer of free passage to anywhere in the world for informa-tion on a man resembling (and presumed to be) Grivas.

Terrorists killed retired British Army Lt. Col. Guy Thompson, 56, a director of Cyprus Airways, near Monarga May 14. EOKA leaflets May 12 called for the "execution" of "Gauleiter Sir John" (Gov. Harding). EOKA men in Nicosia Apr. 14 had killed Asst. Police Supt. Kyriakos Aristotelou, 33, government witness at the Karaolis trial. A British RAF man was killed May 16, and 3 suspects were captured by helicopter. (All shipping off northern Cyprus was banned by Britain May 18 to shut off guerrilla sources of weapons.)

Turkish Cypriots rioted and damaged Greek Cypriot shops and windows in several towns May 24-25. The communal rioting was renewed May 27 and the British announced plans to separate the rival quarters in Nicosia with barbed wire.

(Reports released by British authorities on terrorist incidents between May 16 and June 12 listed 14 British soldiers killed and 49 wounded, 2 British civilians dead and one wounded, 5 Turkish Cypriot policemen killed, 12 Cypriot civilians dead and 51 wounded. British military dispatches for the period reported 28 EOKA men captured. 19 British soldiers were burned to death and 68 injured June 18 when forest fires of unknown origin swept the Troodos Mountains during a British drive there against EOKA terrorists.)

U.S. official slain — U.S. Vice Consul William Pierce Boteler, 26, was killed and 3 other U.S. consular workers injured in Nicosia June 18 by a Cypriot terrorist bomb thrown into a restaurant in the Greek section of the city. This was the first killing of an American in the 14 months of Cypriot violence. The U.S. State Department June 19 denounced Boteler's killing and called Cypriot violence "blind and senseless."

More rebels executed — 3 more Greek Cypriot rebels were hanged in Nicosia Aug. 9. One was put to death for the shooting of a Turkish Cypriot policeman Apr. 23. The other 2 had killed a British soldier Dec. 15, 1955. EOKA Aug. 3 threatened the retaliatory execution of retired British civil servant John A. Cremer, 78, who had been kidnapped in Kyrenia Aug. 1. But Cremer was freed unharmed Aug. 5 after the 3 condemned terrorists appealed for his release.

EOKA Truce Short-Lived

EOKA rebels Aug. 17, 1956 announced a suspension of their attacks on British forces. EOKA urged the cease-fire to test British promises of renewed negotiations after a cessation of hostilities. The EOKA appeal warned, however, that if the offer were ignored, "operations will be resumed on a fiercer and more intensive scale."

Cyprus Gov. Harding said Aug. 18 that the EOKA truce offer could provide "an opportunity to make a fresh start" on negotiations for a measure of Cypriot self-rule. The acting ethnarch of the Greek Orthodox Church on Cyprus, Bishop Anthimos of Kitium, said Aug. 17 that the next move was up to Britain. He urged the British to permit the return of exiled Archbishop Makarios as a prelude to negotiations.

Reports from Cyprus Aug. 16 linked the EOKA truce offer to the replacement of EOKA leader George Grivas by Anargyros Karadimas, reportedly the EOKA's new chief under the traditional Cypriot rebel name "Dighenis."

EOKA's truce bid was followed by an offer of amnesty announced by Harding Aug. 22. Under Harding's proposal, rebels had 3 weeks in which to surrender their arms. Those who gave up had the choice of being deported to Greece and losing British citizenship or remaining on Cyprus to face trial for any violent crimes they might have committed while serving with EOKA.

EOKA leaflets, signed by "Dighenis, the leader," rejected the British amnesty offer Aug. 23. The leaflets, scattered in Nicosia, said: "As the military leader of the fighting Cypriot people, to the demand for surrender I answer no — come and get us." The leaflets warned that if Britain had not returned Archbishop Makarios for renewed negotiations by Aug. 27, EOKA would "regain freedom of action." EOKA leaflets circulated Aug. 28 said that "debate is useless." The bombing of British soldiers' homes in Larnaca Aug. 28 and Nicosia Aug. 29 apparently ended the truce.

British Colonial Secy. Lennox-Boyd charged in London Aug. 26 that captured EOKA documents and parts of George Grivas' diary proved that Makarios was the "personal director" of the Cypriot revolt. The British government was reported Aug. 29 to have decided, on the basis of information contained in the documents, not to resume negotiations with Makarios. The documents also prompted British officials to place Bishop Anthimos under house arrest Aug. 26 and to arrest Ethnarchy Secy. Nicos Kranidiotis Sept. 5.

EOKA forces officially put an end to their truce and resumed attacks Aug. 30. Among the incidents reported through Sept. 4: Mines damaged a British tank landing ship in Famagusta harbor Aug. 30. A British policeman, 2 extremists and a bystander were killed in the escape of an EOKA fighter from a Nicosia hospital Aug. 31. Terrorist bombs damaged British Middle East Command Headquarters in Episkopi Sept. 1. Time bombs wrecked the British colonial government printing office in Nicosia Sept. 2, and an unarmed policeman was killed. A British captain was wounded and a Turkish Cypriot killed by EOKA gunfire in Larnaca Sept. 4.

New British Constitutional Proposal

British jurist Lord Radcliffe went to Cyprus July 16, 1956, on Prime Min. Eden's orders, to hold talks on drafting a new Cyprus constitution. Eden had told the House of Commons July 12 that a "liberal" constitution to protect Cyprus' Greek majority and Turkish minority would be put into effect when "terrorism has been overcome and law and order restored." Before Radcliffe returned to Britain Aug. 2, Commons July 19 had defeated, 319-246, a Laborite censure motion against Eden's Cyprus policy. (A previous Laborite censure motion on Eden's Cyprus policy had been defeated in Commons May 14 by 314-236 vote after Colonial Secy. Lennox-Boyd told the opposition that the 1951 Labor government had refused Greek demands for *enosis*.)

The Cypriot Orthodox Church's Ethnarchy Council had rejected Britain's offer of a new constitution July 13. The council said that "Greek Cypriots will continue to press for...self-determination." The church statement said that Archbishop Makarios "alone can discuss the terms" for a new constitution. The council accused Britain of "taking refuge behind another power," presumably Turkey, and of encouraging Turkish opposition to Cypriot self-determination.

Turkish Premier Adnan Menderes had said July 12 that Turkey had made no proposals on Cyprus and would make none until "terrorism in Cyprus" and "the pressure of Greece" had been ended. A July 2 Turkish note to Britain was said to have rejected British plans for Cypriot self-rule and to have demanded protection for Turkish Cypriots under British rule. British Foreign Secy. Selwyn Lloyd said July 7 that any "solution which may be put forward" must "take account of Turkey's position." Menderes reportedly had charged July 2 that Greece "has not hesitated to imperil the future of NATO, the [Greek-Turk-Yugoslav] Balkan Pact and good relations with Britain and Turkey over the Cyprus problem." Greek Foreign Min. Evangelos Averoff-Tossizza July 3 charged Turkey with distortion of the Cyprus issue. He affirmed Greece's "good will" toward its allies and said Greece would accept any "reasonably" termed Cyprus settlement.

Terrorism, Arrests & Riots

British officials announced Jan. 1, 1957 that EOKA terrorists had killed 201 persons, including 80 Britons, in 1956. The
British reported 500 people injured, including 224 Britons, by
terrorists in Cyprus. 521 major and 451 minor EOKA bombings
were listed, together with 440 attempted bombings, in 1956.
(EOKA terrorists killed 2 more British soldiers Feb. 2 and 4.)

British security forces Feb. 5 reported the capture of 189 terrorists and EOKA members in an islandwide roundup.
Anargyros Karadimas and Polykarpos Georghadjis, aides to
EOKA leader George Grivas, were reported captured Jan. 24. 34
Greek Cypriot civilians and 7 Greek priests were arrested Feb. 7-
17 on charges of aiding EOKA. British security forces killed 4
Cypriots in fighting Feb. 7-17. General strikes called by EOKA
to focus world attention on Cyprus during the scheduled UN
debate paralyzed the island Feb. 11 and 18-20.

Turkish Cypriots had rioted and set fires in the Greek section of Nicosia Jan. 20 in retaliation for the killing of a Turkish
policeman by Greek Cypriots Jan. 19. Turkish Cypriots rioted
Feb. 3 in Famagusta, where they attacked a church and hospital,
killed one Greek Cypriot and injured 11 other Greek Cypriots.
Greek Foreign Min. Evangelos Averoff-Tossizza, in a letter to
the UN General Assembly's Political Committee Jan. 21, had
charged that anti-Greek "Turkish gangs" were being organized
by the British. (Volkan, the Turkish Cypriot underground
organization, announced Jan. 26 that it would support British
suppression of the Cypriot *enosis* movement.)

UN Urges New Negotiations

The UN General Assembly, by 55-0 vote (Afghanistan
abstaining) Feb. 26, 1957, adopted a resolution calling for the
resumption of negotiations toward a "just solution" of the
Cyprus dispute. The resolution, an Indian compromise that
would permit renewed British-Greek-Turkish-Cypriot talks on
the island's future, had been approved in the Assembly's Political

Committee Feb. 22 by 76-0 vote (Afghanistan and Panama abstaining). It urged the re-establishment of "an atmosphere of peace and freedom of expression" on Cyprus as an indispensable condition for settlement. These 4 draft resolutions on Cyprus had been withdrawn in the Political Committee Feb. 22 following the committee's approval of the Indian compromise: (1) a British draft demanding UN action to halt alleged Greek support of Cypriot terrorists; (2 & 3) 2 Greek resolutions asking for a declaration of self-determination for Cyprus and a UN inquiry on the dispute; (4) a Panamanian draft urging a UN investigation of counter-charges of Greek terrorism and British repression on the island.

British State Min. Allan Noble had told the Political Committee Feb. 18 that Cypriot terrorists had been "organized and financed" with Greek aid and "exploited by" Greece. Selim Sarper, Turkish UN delegation chief, charged Feb. 18 that the terrorists had been used for a "campaign of hate" against Cyprus' Turkish minority. Greek Foreign Min. Evangelos Averoff-Tossizza charged Feb. 19 that British agents had made "fake deliveries" of arms to Cyprus to bolster accusations of Greek intervention. James J. Wadsworth, deputy U.S. representative to the UN, urged Feb. 20 that the conflicting resolutions be dropped to avoid "further aggravating" of the Cyprus dispute.

Gov. Harding hailed the final UN resolution Feb. 23 because it urged "the cessation of terrorism" as indispensable to a Cyprus settlement. The outlawed Cypriot Communist Party (AKEL) indorsed the resolution Feb. 23 and demanded the return of exiled Archbishop Makarios for renewed negotiations. (A Laborite motion proposing Makarios' return to Cyprus was defeated in the British House of Commons Feb. 19 by 307-253 vote).

Makarios Released from Seychelles

The British government Mar. 28, 1957 ordered Archbishop Makarios released from detention in the Seychelle Islands, where he had been held since his deportation from Cyprus Mar. 9, 1956. British Colonial Secy. Alan T. Lennox-Boyd told the House of

Commons Mar. 28 that Makarios and the 3 Orthodox churchmen exiled with him would be freed to go anywhere except to Cyprus. (Makarios went to Athens Apr. 17.) Boyd said Makarios Mar. 22 had accepted British offers of his release, made Mar. 20, if he would call for an end to EOKA's terrorist campaign for *enosis*. Britain Mar. 20 offered safe conduct out of Cyprus to EOKA commander George Grivas and any other foreign citizens serving with the group.

Makarios' statement, issued Mar. 28, appealed to EOKA "to declare the cessation of all operations, given that the British government will show a spirit of understanding by abolishing simultaneously the present state of emergency" on Cyprus. Makarios noted the UN resolution calling for the resumption of talks on Cyprus. He said he "would be extremely sorry if the road to peace thus now opened were to be blocked." But Makarios told newsmen Mar. 29 that he was "not prepared to negotiate for the political future of Cyprus until I am allowed to return" to Cyprus.

(The Marquess of Salisbury, leader of the House of Lords and Lord President of the Council, a cabinet post with responsibility for atomic affairs, resigned both positions Mar. 29 in protest against Makarios' release. Salisbury, who retained his House of Lords seat, was succeeded in the 2 posts by the Earl of Home, state secretary for Commonwealth relations. Responsibility for atomic energy was ordered transferred to Prime Min. Harold Macmillan.)

EOKA terrorists had offered Mar. 14 to suspend operations in their campaign for *enosis* if Britain ended Makarios' exile. EOKA said its offer was made in "the spirit of the Feb. 26 [UN] resolution" and to "facilitate the resumption of negotiations between Britain and the real representative of the Cypriot people, Archbishop Makarios." British Colonial Secy. Lennox-Boyd replied Mar. 20 that Makarios would be freed but not permitted to return to Cyprus immediately unless he called for cessation of all EOKA violence.

Lennox-Boyd, in a statement to the House of Commons following talks in London Mar. 19 between Prime Min. Macmillan and Gov. Harding, said that Britain was ready to accept a Dec.

1956 NATO offer to mediate the Cyprus dispute among Britain, Greece and Turkey. Greek Premier Constantine Karamanlis rejected NATO mediation Mar. 20; he held that negotiations must be between Britain and the Cypriot people. Turkish Premier Adnan Menderes, interviewed Mar. 19 for the *N.Y. Herald Tribune,* said that he distrusted the EOKA truce offer and would not enter into talks with Karamanlis. Menderes opposed the release of Makarios before the eradication of the EOKA.

The Turkish government, acting in protest against Greek support of Makarios, closed the Greek-Turkish Hellenic Union in Ankara Apr. 20 and arrested its secretary on espionage charges. The Greek government was reported Apr. 19 to have rejected formal Turkish protests against the welcome given Makarios on his arrival in Athens Apr. 17. Makarios, greeted by Foreign Min. Evangelos Averoff-Tossizza and Greek Archbishop Dorotheos and supported by Athenian demonstrations in favor of *enosis,* had left the Seychelles Islands Apr. 6.

Foot Replaces Harding as Governor

The British government Oct. 21, 1957 appointed Sir Hugh Mackintosh Foot to succeed Sir John Harding as governor of Cyprus at the expiration of Harding's term Dec. 1. Foot, governor of Jamaica since 1951, arrived in Cyprus Dec. 2 to assume his post. Laborite demands that Harding be replaced by a civilian had been rejected by the British House of Commons July 15 on a 326-260 confidence vote backing Prime Min. Macmillan's Cyprus policies.

UN Again Rejects Greek Call for Self-Rule

The UN General Assembly voted Dec. 14, 1957, by 31-23 (24 abstentions, including the U.S.; 24 votes short of required 2/3 majority), to reject a Greek resolution calling for self-determination for Cyprus. The resolution, backed by the Soviet bloc, Arab-Asian and some Latin-American states, had been approved Dec. 12 for Assembly passage by a 33-20 vote (25 abstentions, including the U.S.) of the Assembly's Political Committee. Greek, British and Turkish delegates expressed satisfaction with the Assembly vote Dec. 14. Greek Foreign Min. Averoff-Tossizza's appeal for Cypriot self-rule had been opposed earlier the same day by British State Min. Allan H. P. Noble as a disguised plea for Greek annexation of Cyprus. (Noble, speaking at the close of the Political Committee's Cyprus debate Dec. 9-11, reiterated British pledges for "the immediate introduction of liberal self-government to be followed, when circumstances were more propitious, by self-determination." Noble Dec. 9 had expressed British willingness to renew negotiations with Greece, Turkey and the "peoples of Cyprus.")

U.S. Amb.-to-UN Henry Cabot Lodge told the Political Committee Dec. 12 that the U.S. had abstained on the Cyprus resolution because Cyprus was "not the kind of problem which can be solved by [UN] deliberations in the absence of agreement among the parties." Lodge had urged the committee Dec. 10 to "be moderate and avoid actions and statements which might make a solution harder."

Greek Cypriot riots Dec. 7-15 apparently were timed to coincide with the UN action on the Cyprus issue. 75 persons, including 12 policemen, were injured and 150 arrested Dec. 9 in clashes between Greek Cypriots and British security forces throughout the island. The violence followed in response to an EOKA call for a general strike against British rule. One Cypriot was reported killed and 2 others and 4 British soldiers wounded in Famagusta rioting following the UN General Assembly vote Dec. 15. Col. George Grivas had warned in leaflets distributed Nov. 29 that EOKA's "war" with Britain would continue until Britain "grants self-determination." Grivas had pledged Nov. 22 that he would retire from political life when EOKA's aims were attained.

Leaflets circulated on Cyprus Nov. 28 announced that Volkan, the Turkish Cypriot underground organization, had been replaced by a new "Turkish resistance organization."

Terrorist bombs exploded Dec. 13 in the U.S. Information Service offices in Athens and at the U.S Air Force's Hellenikon airfield, wounding 4 USAF and one Greek airmen.

Violence Follows Turkish Cypriot Demand for Partition

Cyprus, already torn by strife since 1955, was swept by increased turmoil in 1958 as the Turkish Cypriots took to the streets and fought with Greek Cypriots and British security forces. The violence was sparked by Turkish Cypriot demands for partition of the island into Greek and Turkish zones. The Turkish government entered the dispute by vigorously pressing for these claims on the political front.

The first Turkish Cypriot outbreak occurred Jan. 26-28 in Nicosia, where fighting broke out with British forces. 8 Turkish Cypriots were killed, and 40 policemen and soldiers were wounded.

The violence followed talks on the Cyprus issue by Turkish Premier Adnan Menderes and Foreign Min. Fatin Rustu Zorlu with British Foreign Secy. Selwyn Lloyd in Ankara Jan 25. Gov. Sir Hugh Foot, who had returned to the island Jan. 17 after talks in London, flew to Ankara Jan. 26 to join Lloyd in the discussions. Zorlu asserted Jan. 30 that Britain had agreed to "take no action to settle the Cyprus question without Turkish approval." But the British Foreign Office denied Zorlu's contention the same day. The Foreign Office affirmed that Britain alone remained "directly responsible" for "law and order and for the political evolution" of Cyprus.

Turkish Cypriot leader Fazil Kutchuk went to Ankara later. Returning to Cyprus Feb. 3, he told Turkish Cypriots that "the Greek idea of *enosis* is buried once and for all." Kutchuk claimed full Turkish government support for his party's demand for the partition of Cyprus. 5,000 Turkish Cypriots, meeting in Nicosia, agreed Apr. 27 to form separate Turkish municipalities in Cyprus' major towns and to withhold taxes from Greek Cypriot-led local councils.

Leftist Greek Cypriot union members clashed with rightists in Limassol and Famagusta May 26 while protesting the murder of 3 Turkish and one Greek Cypriot unionists May 24-26. Leftists blamed EOKA terrorists for the killings.

Turkish Cypriots rioted and attacked Greeks in Nicosia and Larnaca June 6-10 in what was described as the worst strife among Cypriots since Greeks began their 3-year campaign against British rule. 6 persons were killed and more than 90 injured before fighting was halted June 10 by an island-wide curfew ordered June 9 by Gov Foot. There was fighting in Nicosia June 8 after Turkish Cypriots demonstrated there in a demand for partition of the island and in protest against the bombing June 7 of the Turkish Information Office in Nicosia.

A 3,000-man parachute brigade was ordered to Cyprus from England June 12-14 to reinforce an estimated 10,000-12,000 British combat troops already on the island.

Greek-Turkish rioting and arson were reported in Nicosia and Limassol June 11, and 2 Greeks were killed by Turkish gunfire near Nicosia June 12. 6 Greek Cypriots were killed by Turks June 13 near Geunyeli, north of Nicosia, after the Greeks had been detained, disarmed and then freed near a Turkish area by British security forces.

A Turkish Foreign Ministry communique issued in Ankara June 11 denied responsibility for the Greek-Turkish strife on Cyprus and blamed Britain for having caused bloodshed by efforts to press Turkish and Greek Cypriots into "undesired cooperation."

Renewed fighting between Greek and Turkish Cypriots July 10-14 brought to 52 the number of Cypriot civilians killed since Greek-Turkish strife began June 6. Among incidents reported: 5 persons killed July 10 during an attack on a convent near Aradypou; 3 Cypriots, including a Turkish policeman, killed July 11; 7 persons, 5 of them Turkish Cypriots on an ambushed bus, killed July 12; 4 persons killed July 13 and one July 14. 2 British soldiers were killed in Famagusta July 8, apparently in retaliation for the British killing of 2 Cypriots July 3 in Averou.

Gov. Foot appealed to Greek and Turkish Cypriots July 14 to halt a threatened "general conflict between the 2 communities" that could "destroy the island." A joint appeal signed July 12 by Foot, Mayor Themistocles Dervis of Nicosia and Dr. Rauf Denktash, a Turkish Cypriot leader, had asked that Cypriots cooperate to end the violence. The Turkish Cypriot underground TMT, however, warned July 14 that "until now we were only shooting Greeks who were our enemies; henceforth we will shoot any Greek." (In leaflets circulated Feb. 2, TMT had called for increased "passive resistance" to British rule.)

Gov. Foot disclosed July 23 that 1,450 Greek and 44 Turkish Cypriots had been arrested in a 48-hour roundup of all known or suspected terrorists July 21-22. Foot said that the islandwide roundup had been made necessary by (a) Greek-Turkish strife in which 95 persons had been killed and 170 wounded since early June, and (b) rumors of an impending offensive by EOKA terrorists. He announced that TMT had also been banned for incitement to terrorism. British authorities July 22 had authorized (1) a 48-hour suspension of all overseas and most internal communications, (2) the rearrest of political prisoners released under recent amnesty provisions, and (3) the reintroduction of laws permitting detainees to be held without trial. An islandwide nighttime curfew, lifted July 16, had been reimposed July 21 after 7 Cypriots were killed July 18 and 5 killed and 23 wounded July 20-21. Violence was resumed despite the mass arrests, with 5 Turkish and 5 Greek Cypriots reported killed July 28-29.

New Truce

EOKA commander George Grivas Aug. 5 declared a military truce with Turkish Cypriots and British security forces. Grivas, who ordered EOKA members to halt "all operations," warned by leaflet that his organization would resume its fight for *enosis* "if provocation by the British and the Turks continues after our truce." The outlawed Turkish Cypriot TMT underground organization accepted the EOKA truce offer Aug. 5 and ordered "all armed groups to stop activities until further notice." 2 previous EOKA truce offers, in Aug. 1956 and Mar. 1957, had ended in failure.

The EOKA-TMT truce followed peace appeals by Premiers Karamanlis of Greece July 30, Macmillan of Britain July 31 and Menderes of Turkey Aug. 1. 152 people had been killed in the Cypriot violence since June 7. 25 of them, including 2 British soldiers, had died in clashes that took place Aug. 1-4.

Greece Cuts Military Ties with Turkey

The Greek government, acting after continued fighting between Greek and Turkish Cypriots, announced June 15, 1958 that it had severed all military links with Turkey under NATO's Southeast Europe Command. Athens dispatches reported that Greek army units along the Turkish frontier had been alerted to reports of Turkish army concentrations. Evacuation of Greek personnel from NATO headquarters in Izmir, Turkey was completed by a Greek airlift June 14.

The Greek action led to a decision by the NATO Permanent Council Oct. 29 to abandon efforts to arrange British-Greek-Turkish talks on the Cyprus dispute. NATO spokesmen made clear that Secy. Gen. Paul-Henri Spaak would not continue his attempted mediation of the problem after Greek refusal to attend Cyprus talks without prior political guarantees. A British Foreign Office White Paper asserted Oct. 31 that Spaak's preparations for a Cyprus conference had been nearly completed when halted by the Greek rejection.

U.S. State Department spokesman Lincoln White denied Oct. 30 that NATO had ended all efforts to end the Cyprus crisis. He asserted that the U.S. had agreed to attend, with observer status, any NATO parley on Cyprus.

The NATO Permanent Council had met in Paris June 10 but refused to make public any stand it may have on the Greek-Turkish dispute. The meeting had been requested by Greece June 8 to consider charges that anti-Greek Cypriot riots in Cyprus had been instigated by the Turkish government.

Britain Offers New Partnership Plan

British Prime Min. Macmillan invited the Greek and Turkish governments June 19, 1958 to join Britain and the Greek and Turkish Cypriot communities in "an adventure in partnership" designed to bring Cyprus under limited tripartite control with self-government for its Greek and Turkish populations. A modified version of the plan was put into effect Oct. 1.

Macmillan, presenting his new plan for Cyprus to the House of Commons, urged the establishment of joint control over Cyprus during a 7-year period in which the island's legal and international status would remain unchanged. He pledged that Britain "would be prepared, at the appropriate time," to "share the sovereignty of the island with...[its] Greek and Turkish allies." The British plan envisaged the preparation of a Cypriot constitution containing these major provisions: (1) the Greek Cypriot majority (416,000) and Turkish Cypriot minority (92,000) would exercise full autonomy in communal affairs through separate houses of representatives with "final legislative authority" in this sphere: (2) "authority for internal administration, other than communal affairs," would be vested in a council, presided over by a British governor and containing representatives of the Greek and Turkish governments and 6 elected ministers drawn from the communal legislatures (4 Greek Cypriots, 2 Turkish Cypriots); (3) "external affairs, defense and internal security" would be "specifically reserved to the governor, acting after consultation with the representatives of the Greek and Turkish governments"; (4) the Greek and Turkish government delegates would "have the right to require any legislation which they consider... discriminatory" to be submitted to "an impartial tribunal."

Macmillan requested that Greece and Turkey name representatives to join with British, Greek and Turkish Cypriot leaders in preparing the new constitution. He offered Cypriots the opportunity to acquire Greek or Turkish nationality while retaining their British citizenship. Promising "progressive steps to relax the emergency regulations" on Cyprus, he offered the eventual return of exiled Cypriot leaders.

Greek Foreign Min. Evangelos Averoff-Tossizza rejected the British plan June 21 and informed British Amb.-to-Greece Sir Roger Allen that Greece would seek UN action to win Cypriot self-determination. Greek Premier Constantine Karamanlis made public June 21 a letter to Prime Min. Macmillan in which he expressed Greek willingness to reopen negotiations on the Cyprus problem. Karamanlis insisted, however, that such talks must be limited to Britain, Greece and Cyprus and deal with "the right of

Cypriots to self-determination." He rejected Turkish participation in any Cyprus negotiations on the ground that Turkey had forfeited all rights on Cyprus by the Lausanne Treaty of 1924, which gave Britain sovereignty over the island.

Archbishop Makarios rejected the Macmillan plan June 20 on the ground that it would continue foreign rule of Cyprus and abridge "the fundamental and inalienable rights...[of Cypriots] to self-determination." Makarios, in a statement issued after he met in Athens with the Cypriot Ethnarchy Council and mayors of Cyprus' 6 largest cities, offered "bilateral talks" between Britain and Cypriot leaders on the question of "genuine...self-government."

Turkish Foreign Min. Fatin Rustu Zorlu June 20 renewed demands for the partition of Cyprus but offered to participate in a high level British-Greek-Turkish meeting that would discuss the British plan as "a conference paper." Softening Turkish insistence on partition as the only way to safeguard Cyprus' Turkish minority, Zorlu said that "it is quite possible to fuse together the principles of partition and partnership" to achieve a "well-developed plan" for a Cyprus settlement.

EOKA leaflets, allegedly signed by George Grivas, denounced the British plan June 26 as "a new monstrosity" designed to perpetuate British rule of Cyprus. Manifestos issued Aug. 21 by EOKA and the leftist Pan-Cyprian Labor Federation rejected Britain's revised plan. EOKA warned: "Our island is Greek. We accept no compromise. We demand clear self-determination."

British Plan in Effect

A modified version of Britain's 7-year "partnership" plan for limited Cypriot self-rule was put into effect Oct. 1 despite an islandwide general strike called by Greek Cypriots in opposition to the plan. The modified version, announced by Britain Aug. 15, called for: (1) the eventual creation of a unified Cypriot legislature; (2) invitations to the Greek and Turkish governments to appoint liaison representatives directly to the British governor of Cyprus; (3) permission for the creation of separate Greek and

Turkish municipal councils; (4) the delay of proposals for dual British-Greek or British-Turk citizenship for Cypriots.

Greek Premier Constantine Karamanlis informed Macmillan Aug. 19 that Greece would not support the British plan or name an envoy to the British governor. Karamanlis denounced the inclusion of Turkey in the Cyprus plan and the provision for the creation of separate Greek and Turkish legislatures.

Archbishop Makarios rejected the modified British plan Aug. 16.

Turkey accepted the plan by appointing a representative to Gov. Foot. Burhan Ishin assumed this post Oct. 1 as Foot's special adviser on Turkish affairs.

The revised British plan had grown out of talks Prime Min. Macmillan held with Greek and Turkish officials in Athens and Ankara Aug. 9. The British leader reportedly won Turkish support for an extension of the Cyprus truce and for the application of limited Cypriot self-government in return for recognition of Turkey's continued interest in Cyprus. Macmillan returned to London Aug. 12 after a brief stop in Nicosia for meetings with Greek Cypriot leaders Themistocles Dervis and Charilaos Demetriades and Turkish Cypriot leaders Fazil Kutchuk and Rauf Denktash.

CREATION OF THE REPUBLIC 1959-60

Continued negotiations among all parties to the Cyprus dispute finally produced an agreement in 1959 on the establishment of a republic. A series of accords, announced in Zurich Feb. 11 by the Greek and Turkish foreign ministers, was signed in London Feb. 19 by those 2 ministers and by representatives of Britain and the Greek and Turkish Cypriot communities.

In addition to the establishment of the republic, the pacts provided for a Treaty of Guarantee, under which Britain, Greece and Turkey guaranteed the independence and territorial integrity of the new nation, and a Treaty of Alliance between Greece, Turkey and Cyprus, which provided for a system of common defense against any aggression directed against the island republic. A British amnesty clause in the accords provided for the granting of safe-conduct to Greece of EOKA leader George Grivas. Grivas vowed that he would continue to campaign for enosis.

Cyprus was declared a republic Aug. 16, 1960 under the presidency of Archbishop Makarios and the vice presidency of Fazil Kutchuk, leader of the Turkish Cypriot community.

Agreement to Establish a Republic

Premiers Constantine Karamanlis of Greece and Adnan Menderes of Turkey announced Feb. 11, 1959 in Zurich, Switzerland that they had agreed on a compromise plan for settling the Cyprus dispute. The Greek-Turkish accord provided for establishment in 1960 of a Cypriot republic independent of Britain, Greece and Turkey. Britain, however, would retain its Cyprus bases, and a mixed Greek-Turkish garrison on Cyprus would guarantee the maintenance of the agreement.

A joint communique issued by Karamanlis and Menderes after they had met Feb. 5-11 said that Foreign Mins. Evangelos Averoff-Tossizza of Greece and Fatin Rustu Zorlu of Turkey had been ordered to London to inform Britain of the agreement. Karamanlis and Menderes expressed certainty that the accord would "lead to a final solution of the Cyprus question" in further talks with Britain. They asserted that "the cause of the unity and welfare of Cyprus" had emerged "victorious" from the Zurich talks.

A document embodying an "agreed foundation for the final settlement of the problem of Cyprus" was signed in London Feb. 19 by Prime Mins. Macmillan of Britain, Menderes of Turkey and Karamanlis of Greece. The agreement confirmed provisions of the Feb. 11 accord. It also was signed by Archbishop Makarios for the Greek Cypriot community and by Fazil Kutchuk for the Turkish Cypriot community. Final terms of the agreement, made public Feb. 23 in a British White Paper and in simultaneous Greek and Turkish government announcements, had been reached in London talks Feb. 17-18 among Makarios, Kutchuk and Foreign Mins. Selwyn Lloyd of Britain, Zorlu of Turkey and Averoff-Tossizza of Greece.

The Zurich accords provided for the creation of a Cypriot republic by Feb. 19, 1960. The text of the Zurich agreement:

"(1) The state of Cyprus shall be a republic with a presidential regime, the president being Greek and the vice president Turkish elected by universal suffrage by the Greek and Turkish communities of the island respectively.

"(2) The official languages of the Republic of Cyprus shall be Greek and Turkish. Legislative and administrative instruments and documents shall be drawn up and promulgated in the 2 official languages.

"(3) The Republic of Cyprus shall have its own flag of neutral design and color, chosen jointly by the president and the vice president of the republic.

"Authorities and communities shall have the right to fly the Greek and Turkish flags on holidays at the same time as the flag of Cyprus.

"The Greek and Turkish communities shall have the right to celebrate Greek and Turkish national holidays.

"(4) The president and the vice president shall be elected for a period of 5 years.

"In the event of absence, impediment, or vacancy of their posts, the president and the vice president shall be replaced by the president and the vice president of the House of Representatives respectively.

"In the event of a vacancy in either post, the election of new incumbents shall take place within a period of not more than 45 days.

"The president and the vice president shall be invested by the House of Representatives, before which they shall take an oath of loyalty and respect for the constitution. For this purpose the House of Representatives shall meet within 24 hours after its constitution.

"(5) Executive authority shall be vested in the president and the vice president. For this purpose they shall have a Council of Ministers composed of 7 Greek ministers and 3 Turkish ministers. The ministers shall be designated respectively by the president and the vice president, who shall appoint them by an instrument signed by them both.

"The ministers may be chosen from outside the House of Representatives.

"Decisions of the Council of Ministers shall be taken by an absolute majority.

"Decisions so taken shall be promulgated immediately by the president and the vice president by publication in the *Official Gazette.*

"However, the president and the vice president shall have the right of final veto and the right to return the decisions of the Council of Ministers under the same conditions as those laid down for laws and decisions of the House of Representatives.

"(6) Legislative authority shall be vested in a House of Representatives elected for a period of 5 years by universal suffrage of each community separately in the proportion of 70% for the Greek community and 30% for the Turkish community, this proportion being fixed independently of statistical data. (*N.B.* — The number of representatives shall be fixed by mutual agreement between the communities.)

"The House of Representatives shall exercise authority in all matters other than those expressly reserved to the Communal Chambers. In the event of a conflict of authority, such conflict shall be decided by the Supreme Constitutional Court, which shall be composed of one Greek, one Turk and one neutral, appointed jointly by the president and the vice president. The neutral judge shall be president of the court.

"(7) Laws and decisions of the House of Representatives shall be adopted by a simple majority of the members present. They shall be promulgated within 15 days if neither the president nor the vice president returns them for reconsideration as provided in (9) below.

"The Constitutional Law, with the exception of its basic articles, may be modified by a majority comprising 2/3 of the Greek members and 2/3 of the Turkish members of the House of Representatives.

"Any modification of the electoral law, and the adoption of any law relating to the municipalities and of any law imposing duties or taxes, shall require a simple majority of the Greek and Turkish members of the House of Representatives taking part in the vote and considered separately.

"On the adoption of the budget, the president and the vice president may exercise their right to return it to the House of Representatives if in their judgment any question of discrimination arises. If the House maintains its decisions, the president and the vice president shall have the right of appeal to the Supreme Constitutional Court.

"(8) The president and the vice president, separately and conjointly, shall have the right of final veto on any law or decision concerning foreign affairs, except the participation of the Republic of Cyprus in international organizations and pacts of alliance in which Greece and Turkey both participate, or concerning defense and security as defined in Annex I [below].

"(9) The president and the vice president of the republic shall have, separately and conjointly, the right to return all laws and decisions ... to the House of Representatives within a period of not more than 15 days for reconsideration. The House of Representatives shall pronounce within 15 days on any matter so returned. If the House of Representatives maintains its decisions, the president and the vice president shall promulgate the law or decision in question within the time-limits fixed for the promulgation of laws and decisions.

"Laws and decisions which are considered by the president or the vice president to discriminate against either of the 2 communities shall be submitted to the Supreme Constitutional Court, which may annul or confirm the law or decision, or return it to the House of Representatives for reconsideration, in whole or in part. The law or decision shall not become effective until the Supreme Constitutional Court or, where it has been returned, the House of Representatives, has taken a decision on it.

"(10) Each community shall have its Communal Chamber composed of a number of representatives which it shall itself determine.

"The Communal Chambers shall have the right to impose taxes and levies on members of their community to provide for their needs and for the needs of bodies and institutions under their supervision.

"The Communal Chambers shall exercise authority in all religious, educational, cultural and teaching questions and questions of personal status. They shall exercise authority in questions where the interests and institutions are of a purely communal nature, such as sporting and charitable foundations, bodies and associations, producers, and consumers' cooperatives and credit establishments, created for the purpose of promoting the welfare of one of the communities. (*N.B.* — It is understood that the provisions of this paragraph cannot be interpreted in such a way as to prevent the creation of mixed and communal institutions where the inhabitants desire them.)

"These producers' and consumers' cooperatives and credit establishments, which shall be administered under the laws of the republic, shall be subject to the supervision of the Communal Chambers. The Communal Chambers shall also exercise authority in matters initiated by municipalities which are composed of one community only. These municipalities, to which the laws of the republic shall apply, shall be supervised in their functions by the Communal Chambers.

"Where the central administration is obliged to take over the supervision of the institutions, establishments or municipalities mentioned in the 2 preceding paragraphs by virtue of legislation in force, this supervision shall be exercised by officials belonging to the same community as the institution, establishment or municipality in question.

"(11) The Civil Service shall be composed as to 70% of Greeks and as to 30% of Turks.

"It is understood that this quantitative division will be applied as far as practicable in all grades of the Civil Service.

"In regions or localities where one of the 2 communities is in a majority approaching 100%, the organs of the local administration responsible to the central administration shall be composed solely of officials belonging to that community.

"(12) The deputies of the attorney general of the republic, the inspector general, the treasurer and the governor of the issuing bank may not belong to the same community as their principals. The holders of these posts shall be appointed by the president and the vice president of the republic acting in agreement.

"(13) The heads and deputy heads of the armed forces, the gendarmerie, and the police shall be appointed by the president and the vice president of the republic acting in agreement. One of these heads shall be Turkish, and where the head belongs to one of the communities, the deputy head shall belong to the other.

"(14) Compulsory military service may only be instituted with the agreement of the president and the vice president of the Republic of Cyprus.

"Cyprus shall have an army of 2,000 men, of whom 60% shall be Greek and 40% Turkish.

The security forces (gendarmerie and police) shall have a complement of 2,000 men, which may be reduced or increased with the agreement of both the president and the vice president. The security forces shall be composed as to 70% of Greeks and as to 30% of Turks. However, for an initial period this percentage may be raised to a maximum of 40% of Turks (and consequently reduced to 60% of Greeks) in order not to discharge those Turks now serving in the police, apart from the auxiliary police.

"(15) Forces which are stationed in parts of the territory of the republic inhabited, in a proportion approaching 100%, by members of a single community, shall belong to that community.

"(16) A High Court of Justice shall be established which shall consist of 2 Greeks, one Turk and one neutral, nominated jointly by the president and the vice president of the republic.

"The president of the court shall be the neutral judge, who shall have 2 votes.

"This court shall constitute the highest organ of the judicature (appointments, promotions of judges, etc.).

"(17) Civil disputes, where the plaintiff and the defendant belong to the same community, shall be tried by a tribunal composed of judges belonging to that community. If the plaintiff and defendant belong to different communities, the composition of the tribunal shall be mixed and shall be determined by the High Court of Justice.

"Tribunals dealing with civil disputes relating to questions of personal status and to religious matters, which are reserved to the competence of the Communal Chambers under Point 10, shall be composed solely of judges belonging to the community concerned. The composition and status of these tribunals shall be determined according to the law drawn up by the Communal Chamber, and they shall apply the law drawn up by the Communal Chamber.

"In criminal cases the tribunal shall consist of judges belonging to the same community as the accused. If the injured party belongs to another community, the composition of the tribunal shall be mixed and shall be determined by the High Court of Justice.

"(18) The president and the vice president of the republic shall each have the right to exercise the prerogative of mercy to persons from their respective communities who are condemned to death. In cases where the plaintiffs and the convicted persons are members of different communities, the prerogative of mercy shall be exercised by agreement between the president and the vice president. In the event of disagreement the vote for clemency shall prevail. When mercy is accorded, the death penalty shall be commuted to life imprisonment.

"(19) In the event of agricultural reform, lands shall be redistributed only to persons who are members of the same community as the expropriated owners.

"Expropriations by the state or the municipalities shall only be carried out on payment of a just and equitable indemnity fixed, in disputed cases, by the tribunals. An appeal to the tribunals shall have the effect of suspending action.

"Expropriated property shall only be used for the purpose for which the expropriation was made. Otherwise the property shall be restored to the owners.

"(20) Separate municipalities shall be created in the 5 largest towns of Cyprus by the Turkish inhabitants of these towns. However:

"(a) In each of the towns a coordinating body shall be set up which shall supervise work which needs to be carried out jointly and shall concern itself with matters which require a degree of cooperation. These bodies shall each be composed of 2 members chosen by the Greek municipalities, 2 members chosen by the Turkish municipalities and a president chosen by agreement between the 2 municipalities.

"(b) The president and the vice president shall examine within 4 years the question whether or not this separation of municipalities in the 5 largest towns shall continue.

"With regard to other localities, special arrangements shall be made for the constitution of municipal bodies, following as far as possible the rule of proportional representation for the 2 communities.

"(21) A treaty guaranteeing the independence, territorial integrity and constitution of the new state of Cyprus shall be concluded between the Republic of Cyprus, Greece, the United Kingdom and Turkey. A treaty of military alliance shall also be concluded between the Republic of Cyprus, Greece, and Turkey.

"These 2 instruments shall have constitutional force. (This last paragraph shall be inserted in the Constitution as a basic article.)

"(22) It shall be recognized that the total or partial union of Cyprus with any other state, or a separatist independence for Cyprus (i.e. the partition of Cyprus into 2 independent states), shall be excluded.

"(23) The Republic of Cyprus shall accord most-favored-nation treatment to Great Britain, Greece and Turkey for all agreements whatever their nature.

"This provision shall not apply to the treaties between the Republic of Cyprus and the United Kingdom concerning the bases and military facilities accorded to the United Kingdom.

"(24) The Greek and Turkish governments shall have the right to subsidize institutions for education, culture, athletics and charity belonging to their respective communities.

"Equally, where either community considers that it has not the necessary number of schoolmasters, professors or priests for the working of its institutions, the Greek and Turkish governments may provide them to the extent strictly necessary to meet their needs.

"(25) One of the following ministries — the Ministry of Foreign Affairs, the Ministry of Defense or the Ministry of Finance — shall be entrusted to a Turk. If the president and the vice president agree, they may replace this system by a system of rotation.

"(26) The new state which is to come into being with the signature of the treaties shall be established as quickly as possible and within a period of not more than 3 months from the signature of the treaties.

"(27) All the above points shall be considered to be basic articles of the Constitution of Cyprus."

Annex. "The defense questions subject to veto under Point 8 of the Basic Structure are as follows: (*a*) Composition and size of the armed forces and credits for them; (*b*) appointments and promotions; (*c*) imports of warlike stores and of all kinds of explosives; (*d*) granting of bases and other facilities to allied countries.

"The security questions subject to veto are as follows: (*a*) Appointments and promotions; (*b*) allocation and stationing of forces; (*c*) emergency measures and martial law; (*d*) police laws.

"(It is provided that the right of veto shall cover all emergency measures or decisions but not those which concern the normal functioning of the police and gendarmerie)."

A British declaration made public Feb. 23 accepted the transfer to the Republic of Cyprus of the sovereignty over all Cypriot territory except that contained in 2 British military enclaves. *The text of the declaration:*

"The government of the United Kingdom of Great Britain & Northern Ireland ... declare:—

"(A) That, subject to the acceptance of their requirements as set out in Section B below, they accept the documents approved by the heads of the governments of Greece and Turkey as the agreed foundation for the final settlement of the problem of Cyprus.

"(B) That, with the exception of 2 areas at (*a*) Akrotiri — Episkopi — Paramali, and (*b*) Dhekelia — Pergamos — Ayios Nikolaos — Xylophagou, which will be retained under full British sovereignty, they are willing to transfer sovereignty over the island of Cyprus to the Republic of Cyprus subject to the following conditions:

"(1) that such rights are secured to the UK government as are necessary to enable the 2 areas aforesaid to be used effectively as military bases, including among others those rights indicated in the Annex attached, and that satisfactory guarantees are given by Greece, Turkey and the Republic of Cyprus for the integrity of the areas retained under British sovereignty and the use and enjoyment by the United Kingdom of the rights referred to above;

"(2) that provision shall be made by agreement for: (i) the protection of the fundamental human rights of the various communities in Cyprus; (ii) the protection of the interests of the members of the public services in Cyprus; (iii) determining the nationality of persons affected by the settlement; (iv) the assumption by the Republic of Cyprus of the appropriate obligations of the present government of Cyprus, including the settlement of claims.

"(C) That the government of the United Kingdom welcome the draft Treaty of Alliance between the Republic of Cyprus, the Kingdom of Greece, and the Republic of Turkey and will cooperate with the parties thereto in the common defense of Cyprus.

"(D) That the Constitution of the Republic of Cyprus shall come into force and the formal signature of the necessary instruments by the parties concerned shall take place at the earliest practicable date, and on that date sovereignty will be transferred to the Republic of Cyprus."

Annex. "The following rights will be necessary in connection with the areas to be retained under British sovereignty:

"(*a*) to continue to use, without restriction or interference, the existing small sites containing military and other installations and to exercise complete control within these sites, including the right to guard and defend them and to exclude from them all persons not authorized by the UK government;

"(*b*) to use roads, ports and other facilities freely for the movement of personnel and stores of all kinds to and from and between the above-mentioned areas and sites;

"(*c*) to continue to have the use of specified port facilities at Famagusta;

"(*d*) to use public services (such as water, telephone, telegraph, electric power, etc.);

"(*e*) to use from time to time certain localities, which would be specified, for troop training;

"(*f*) to use the airfield at Nicosia, together with any necessary buildings and facilities on or connected with the airfield, to whatever extent is considered necessary by the British authorities for the operation of British military aircraft in peace and war, including the exercise of any necessary operational control of air traffic;

"(*g*) to overfly the territory of the Republic of Cyprus without restriction;

"(*h*) to exercise jurisdiction over British forces to an extent comparable with that provided in Article VII of the Agreement regarding the Status of Forces of Parties to the North Atlantic Treaty, in respect of certain offenses committed within the territory of the Republic of Cyprus;

"(*i*) to employ freely in the areas and sites labor from other parts of Cyprus;

"(*j*) to obtain, after consultation with the government of the Republic of Cyprus, the use of such additional small sites and such additional rights as the United Kingdom may from time to time consider technically necessary for the efficient use of its base areas and installations in Cyprus."

A defense agreement and guarantees against Greek Cypriot efforts to unify with Greece or Turkish Cypriot attempts to partition the island were detailed in 2 draft treaties negotiated in the Feb. 17-18 London talks and made public Feb. 23. The Treaty of Guarantee, to be signed by Cyprus, Britain, Greece and Turkey, contained Cypriot assurances "not to participate ... in any political or economic union with any state" or to permit efforts that would lead to "partition of the island." Britain, Greece and Turkey pledged common action to prevent merger or partition but each retained the right to act alone if common action proved impossible. The treaty consisted of the following 4 articles:

"The Republic of Cyprus of the one part, and Greece, the United Kingdom and Turkey of the other part:

"(I) Considering that the recognition and maintenance of the independence, territorial integrity, and security of the Republic of Cyprus, as established and regulated by the basic articles of its Constitution, are in their common interest;

"(II) Desiring to cooperate to ensure that the provisions of the aforesaid Constitution shall be respected;

"Have agreed as follows:—

"*Article 1.* The Republic of Cyprus undertakes to ensure the maintenance of its independence, territorial integrity and security as well as respect for its constitution.

"It undertakes not to participate, in whole or in part, in any political or economic union with any state whatsoever. With this intent it prohibits all activity tending to promote directly or indirectly either union or partition of the island.

"*Article 2.* Greece, the United Kingdom and Turkey, taking note of the undertakings by the Republic of Cyprus embodied in Article 1, recognize and guarantee the independence, territorial integrity and security of the Republic of Cyprus and also the provisions of the basic articles of its constitution.

"They likewise undertake to prohibit, as far as lies within their power, all activity having the object of promoting directly or indirectly either the union of the Republic of Cyprus with any other state, or the partition of the island.

"*Article 3.* In the event of any breach of the provisions of the treaty, Greece, the United Kingdom and Turkey undertake to consult together with a view to making representations or taking the necessary steps to ensure observance of those provisions.

"In so far as common or concerted action may prove impossible, each of the 3 guaranteeing powers reserves the right to take action with the sole aim of reestablishing the state of affairs established by the treaty.

"*Article 4.* The treaty shall enter into force on signature.

"The high contracting parties undertake to register the treaty at the earliest possible date with the Secretariat of the United Nations."

A Treaty of Alliance, to be signed by Cyprus, Greece and Turkey, pledged common defense measures and committed Greece and Turkey to defend Cyprus against any attack. It provided for the establishment of "a tripartite headquarters" on Cyprus with personnel to include 950 Greek army troops and 650 Turkish army troops and command to be rotated annually among Cypriot, Greek and Turkish generals. *The text of the treaty:*

"(1) The Republic of Cyprus, Greece and Turkey shall cooperate for their common defense and undertake by this treaty to consult together on the problems raised by this defense.

"(2) The high contracting parties undertake to resist any attack or aggression, direct or indirect, directed against the independence and territorial integrity of the Republic of Cyprus.

"(3) In the spirit of this alliance and in order to fulfill the above purpose a tripartite headquarters shall be established on the territory of the Republic of Cyprus.

"(4) Greece shall take part in the headquarters mentioned in the preceding article with a contingent of 950 officers, NCOs and soldiers and Turkey with a contingent of 650 officers, NCOs and soldiers. The president and the vice president of the Republic of Cyprus, acting in agreement, may ask the Greek and Turkish governments to increase or reduce the Greek and Turkish contingents.

"(5) The Greek and Turkish officers mentioned above shall be responsible for the training òf the army of the Republic of Cyprus.

"(6) The command of the tripartite headquarters shall be assumed in rotation and for a period of one year each by a Cypriot, Greek and Turkish general officer, who shall be nominated by the governments of Greece and Turkey and by the president and the vice president of the Republic of Cyprus."

Britain, Greece, Turkey and the 2 Cypriot communities agreed to begin "at once" "measures leading to the transfer of sovereignty in Cyprus." They pledged the creation of a Cyprus constitution and the completion of legislative and presidential elections to assure the establishment of the Cyprus republic by Feb. 19, 1960. *The text of the agreement:*

"(1) All parties to the conference firmly endorse the aim of bringing the constitution (including the elections of president, vice president, and the 3 assemblies) and the treaties into full effect as soon as practicable, and in any case not later than 12 months from today's date (Feb. 19, 1959). Measures leading to the transfer of sovereignty in Cyprus will begin at once.

"(2) The first of these measures will be the immediate establishment of:—

"(a) a joint commission in Cyprus with the duty of completing a draft constitution for the independent Republic of Cyprus, incorporating the basic structure agreed at the Zurich conference. This commission shall be composed of one representative each of the Greek-Cypriot and the Turkish-Cypriot community, one representative nominated by the government of Greece and one representative nominated by the government of Turkey, together with a legal adviser nominated by the foreign ministers of Greece and Turkey; and shall in its work have regard to and scrupulously observe the points contained in the documents of the Zurich conference and fulfill its task in accordance with the principles there laid down;

"(b) a transitional committee in Cyprus with responsibility for drawing up plans for adapting and reorganizing the governmental machinery in Cyprus in preparation for the transfer of authority to the independent Republic of Cyprus. This committee shall be composed of the governor of Cyprus, the leading representative of the Greek community, the leading representative of the Turkish community and other Greek and Turkish Cypriots nominated by the governor after consultation with the 2 leading representatives in such a way as not to conflict with paragraph 5 of the Basic Structure;

"(c) a joint committee in London, composed of a representative of each of the governments of Greece, Turkey and the United Kingdom and one representative each of the Greek-Cypriot and Turkish-Cypriot communities, with the duty of preparing the final treaties giving effect to the conclusions of the London conference. This committee will prepare drafts for submission to governments covering *inter alia* matters arising from the retention of areas in Cyprus under British sovereignty; the provision to the UK government of certain ancillary rights and facilities in the independent Republic of Cyprus; questions of nationality; the treatment of the liabilities of the present government of Cyprus; and the financial and economic problems arising from the creation of an independent Republic of Cyprus.

"(3) The governor will, after consultation with the 2 leading representatives, invite individual members of the transitional committee to assume special responsibilities for particular departments and functions of government. This process will be started as soon as possible and will be progressively extended.

"(4) The headquarters mentioned in Article 4 of the Treaty of Alliance between the Republic of Cyprus, the Kingdom of Greece and the Republic of Turkey will be established 3 months after the completion of the work of the commission referred to in paragraph 2 (a) above and will be composed of a restricted number of officers who will immediately undertake the training of the armed forces of the Republic of Cyprus. The Greek and Turkish contingents will enter the territory of the Republic of Cyprus on the date when sovereignty will be transferred to the republic."

Makarios Feb. 18 had objected strongly to the continued presence of British troops on Cyprus and to the entry of additional Greek and Turkish forces, to the 70%-30% division of the Cypriot House of Representatives between Greek and Turkish Cypriots and to the division of the Cyprus cabinet among 7 Greek and 3 Turkish members. Makarios however, withdrew his protests and signed the accord Feb. 19 when the Greek delegation made clear its refusal to support him.

Prime Min. Macmillan Feb. 19 hailed the Cyprus accords as "a victory for reason and cooperation." He told the House of Commons that the agreements had removed "the source of bitterness and tension" and would "enable us and all our allies and the people of Cyprus to concentrate on working together for peace and freedom." Macmillan's statement was denounced by the opposition. Labor Party leader Hugh Gaitskell said Macmillan's government deserved "particular credit for eating so many words and even inviting Archbishop Makarios to the [London] conference."

State of Emergency Ended, Makarios Returns

The British administration on Cyprus ended a 4-year state of emergency Feb. 22, 1959 and freed 908 political prisoners, reportedly all that remained in the island's 3 detention camps. Gov. Foot said Feb. 24 that amnesty would be granted to all Cypriots imprisoned for terrorist offenses and to Greek and Turkish Cypriot terrorists still at large.

Archbishop Makarios returned to Cyprus Mar. 1 after 3 years in an exile imposed by Britain. Makarios was welcomed on his arrival by Gov. Foot and by an estimated 150,000 Greek Cypriots. Makarios told crowds in Nicosia that the British-Greek-Turkish agreement for establishing an independent Republic of Cyprus had placed "in our hands the responsibility for our future" for "the first time in 3,000 years." Lauding the "numberless heroes" of EOKA and its leader, Col. George T. Grivas, Makarios called for peace between Greek and Turkish Cypriots and for acceptance of the independence accord.

Independence Accords Implemented

Representatives of the 3 governments involved started in Mar. 1959 to implement the accords paving the way for Cyprus' independence.

Agreement on establishment of a 10-member transitional committee to plan the transfer of authority from Britain to a Cypriot provisional government was announced in London Mar. 4 by Gov. Foot, Makarios and Kutchuk. The committee was to have 3 Turkish and 7 Greek Cypriot members. The London agreement was approved by the Greek Chamber of Deputies Feb. 28 by 174-112 vote. The Turkish Grand National Assembly approved it Mar. 4 by 347-138 vote, and the British Parliament approved the agreement Mar. 19.

Foot, Makarios and Kutchuk reached agreement Mar. 27 on distributing government posts among Greek and Turkish Cypriots. Greek Cypriots were to get the ministries of foreign affairs, finance, justice, commerce and industry, interior, communications and public works and labor. Turkish Cypriots were to get the defense, health and agriculture portfolios.

This agreement was followed by the announcement Apr. 5 of the formation of a 12-member cabinet in which Makarios held the post of foreign minister. Several former EOKA leaders held cabinet positions. Among them: Antonis Georghiades, 26, former aide to EOKA commander George Grivas; Tasso Papadopoulos, former leader of PEKA, the EOKA s political branch, and Polycarpos Georghiades, noted terrorist. The Cyprus provisional cabinet: *Foreign Affairs* — Makarios; *Agriculture* — Fazil Plumer; *Deputy Agriculture* — Andreas Azina; *Commerce & Industry* — Paschalis Pascalides; *Communications* — Antonis Georghiades; *Defense* — Osman Orek; *Finance* — Righinos Theocharus; *Deputy Finance* — Memet Nazim; *Health* — Dr. Noyazi Menyera; *Interior* — Tassos Papadapoulos; *Justice* — Glafkos Clerides; *Labor & Social Services* — Polykarpos Georghadjis.

Greek Premier Karamanlis and Foreign Min. Averoff-Tossizza met with Turkish Premier Menderes and Foreign Min. Zorlu in Ankara May 7-9 and reported that they had reached agreements that would permit the formation of an independent Cypriot government within a year as envisaged by the Feb. 19 agreement. A joint Greek-Turkish study group was set up to recommend a uniform local-government system for ethnically mixed Cypriot communities outside Nicosia and 5 other major cities. Greek and Turkish communities were to be segregated geographically and politically in the 6 largest cities. The study group also was to consider how to guarantee the security of 100,000 Turks of Greek origin living in Ankara and of 80,000 Greeks of Turkish origin living in western Thrace.

Bishop Photios of Paphos, Cypriot churchman ranking next after Makarios, abdicated May 7 after being greeted by hostile demonstrations on his return from 3 years of exile as a fugitive from EOKA assassination threats.

Grivas Exiled

Col. George Grivas left Cyprus Mar. 17, 1959 and flew to Athens to begin an exile imposed on him under the British amnesty for EOKA terrorists. Grivas had told newsmen before leaving Nicosia that he was still "fanatically pro-British" but that it was up to Britain "to rebuild this friendship." He was promoted to lieutenant general in the Greek army Mar. 18.

General amnesty measures announced Feb. 27 by Gov. Foot had granted Grivas and other fugitive EOKA leaders freedom from prosecution provided they accepted British safe-conduct to exile in Greece or Turkey. The amnesty was extended to hundreds of Greek Cypriots awaiting trial and serving jail terms for terrorist offenses. It provided that Grivas and designated EOKA leaders remain abroad until permitted to return by the Cypriot republic. 83 political prisoners, first to be freed under the amnesty, were released Feb. 28 from Nicosia Central Prison. Leaflets issued on Cyprus Mar. 9 and signed by Grivas called on EOKA terrorists to cease their struggle and give support to Makarios in founding the Cyprus republic. Grivas said that he was "obliged to order the cessation of the struggle" despite EOKA failure to win *enosis.* He ordered EOKA members to abide by the British-Greek-Turkish pact for Cyprus independence as preferable to continued "national disruption." Grivas issued a similar appeal in a farewell message Mar. 14. He called on all Greek Cypriots to support Makarios. He said that he and other EOKA members had fought only to rid Cyprus "of the chains of slavery." EOKA members began surrendering their weapons, ammunition and explosives to Cypriot police Mar. 13.

During the early months of his exile, Grivas reversed his conciliatory attitude toward Makarios and the independence agreements. Grivas "dissociated" himself July 29 from the London accords. He denounced the accords as an "unforgivable concession to Anglo-Turkish demands." In what was considered an attack on Grivas, Makarios July 26 had denounced "persons" and "circles in Athens" who were "trying to exploit the Cyprus struggle for their own ends." Fazil Kutchuk backed Makarios July 27 and warned Grivas not to interfere in Cyprus' affairs. Makarios openly assailed Grivas Sept. 15 for alleged interference in Cyprus' internal affairs. Makarios said the right to decide Cyprus' political future belonged "only to the Cypriot people." Grivas charged Sept. 19 that Makarios and Greek Prime Min. Constantine Karamanlis had plotted to discredit Grivas with false charges that he had conspired against Makarios' leadership of Cyprus. Makarios and Grivas finally met on Rhodes Oct. 7-9 and agreed to end their dispute over the political future of the Cypriot Republic.

Makarios Elected President

Archbishop Makarios was elected Dec. 13, 1959 as the first president of the Republic of Cyprus. He received 144,501 votes, compared with 71,753 for John Clerides, Communist-supported candidate of the leftist Democratic Front. Fazil Kutchuk had already been elected vice president by acclamation of the Turkish Cypriot community. Only Greek Cypriots voted in the presidential election.

The Democratic Front had been formed Nov. 15 by Clerides and Nicosia Mayor Themistocles Dervis to oppose the allegedly dictatorial methods of Makarios.

Support for Makarios had been expressed by a new right-wing Greek Cypriot political party founded Apr. 9 by EOKA veterans and designated EDMA.

Independence Proclaimed

An independent Republic of Cyprus was proclaimed Aug. 16, 1960 in Nicosia by Sir Hugh Foot, last governor general of the former British crown colony. (The new republic was recognized Aug. 16 by Pres. Eisenhower, who appointed Frazer Wilson, consul general in Nicosia, as U. S. ambassador.)

Treaties guaranteeing the new republic were signed by Archbishop Makarios, Cyprus president-elect, Fazil Kutchuk, vice president-elect, Gov. Gen. Foot, George Christopoulos for Greece and Vedi Turel for Turkey. The treaties forbade the dissolution of the Cypriot republic in favor of union with Greece, pledged Greek-British-Turkish cooperation for Cyprus' development, created a Cypriot-Greek-Turkish military alliance and assured Britain the use of 2 military base areas (99 square miles) on Cyprus. 650 Turkish troops and 950 Greek troops were landed in Famagusta Aug. 16 for garrison duty under the Greek-Turkish-Cypriot treaties a short time after Foot had sailed from the port.

A 50-member Cypriot House of Representatives — 35 elected by Greek Cypriots and 15 by Turkish Cypriots — came into existence Aug. 16 and in turn invested Makarios, Kutchuk and members of Cyprus' first cabinet. The House, elected July 31, was dominated by Makarios' Patriotic Front and Kutchuk's Turkish Cypriot Nationalists. 5 members of the AKEL, the Greek Cypriot Communist party, were elected as Patriotic Front candidates under an agreement with Makarios and were to form the only opposition. All 8 Greek Cypriot and 7 Turkish Cypriot independents who ran for the House were defeated.

The Cyprus cabinet: (Greek Cypriot members) *President* — Archbishop Makarios; *Commerce & Industry* — Andreas Arouzos; *Justice* — Spyros Kyprianou; *Communications & Works* — Andreas Papadapoulos; *Interior* — Polykarpos Georghadjis; *Labor* — Tassos Papadapoulos. (Turkish Cypriot members) *Vice President* — Fazil Kutchuk; *Defense* — Osman Orek; *Agriculture* — Fazil Plumer; *Health* — Noyazi Menyera. The appointments of Spyros Kyprianou as foreign minister and Mrs. Stella Souliotou as justice minister were announced Aug. 22.

A 26-member Greek Cypriot communal chamber and a 30-member Turkish communal chamber had been chosen in separate elections Aug. 6 by the 2 communities.

Public Law Prof. Ernst Forsthoff of Heidelberg University (West Germany) was sworn in Nov. 17 as the neutral president of Cyprus' Supreme Constitutonal Court. Michael Triantafillides, a Greek Cypriot, and Nediati Munir, a Turkish Cypriot, were the other high court judges.

The proclamation of an independent Cyprus republic had been scheduled for Feb. 19 but was delayed when a London conference on implementing 1959 Cyprus independence accords was suspended in disagreement over the size of military enclaves to be retained by Britain on the island. The conference had deadlocked over the question of British bases at its opening session Jan. 16. Convened by British Foreign Secy. Lloyd and attended by Greek Foreign Min. Evangelos Averoff-Tossizza, Turkish Foreign Min. Fatin Rustu Zorlu, Archbishop Makarios and Fazil Kutchuk, the meeting stalled over Makarios' refusal to accept continued British sovereignty over 123-1/2 square miles of Cyprus territory covered by bases near Akrotiri and Dhekelia. A communique issued Jan. 19 disclosed that the conference had been suspended to permit study of the base problem by smaller working groups. The talks were broken off Jan. 28 without an agreement on the issue. A final British offer, made that day by Lloyd, envisaged the tripling of undisclosed British economic aid to Cyprus but refused any reduction of the 123-1/2-square-mile military base area. Britain offered Jan. 26 to permit Cypriot administration of most civil affairs affecting the 2 areas, containing an estimated 1,000 Cypriots. Lloyd told the British Parliament Feb. 1 that his offer was final and that Makarios' demands for reducing the base area to 36 square miles were unacceptable. But an agreement was finally announced July 1. The accords were initialled July 6 by Colonial Undersecy. Julian Amery for Britain, by Makarios and Kutchuk for Cyprus and by representatives of Greece and Turkey.

In a communique issued July 1 after months of talks, Amery, Makarios and Kutchuk reported that the British-Cypriot accord covered (1) the final text of the agreement establishing an independent Cypriot republic, (2) definition of the 2 military base areas to be retained by Britain, (3) pledges of £12 million ($33,600,000) in British aid during the first 5 years of Cypriot independence, (4) payment of an additional £2,340,000 ($6,552,000) by Britain (reportedly for island projects connected with the development of the British military enclaves). Makarios declared July 4 that the new state would remain independent of all military blocs and would try to "become a bridge for good relations between the countries in the Middle East," between Israel and the Arab states as well as between Greece and Turkey.

RENEWAL OF FIGHTING 1963

Cyprus remained relatively calm under the rule of the new independent government for the next 2-1/2 years. Then a new political crisis erupted Jan. 1, 1963. Pres. Makarios had just abolished the municipal councils, and their functions were taken over by the Greek Cypriot-dominated central government. The move angered the Turkish Cypriots Tensions were further exacerbated Nov. 30 when Makarios proposed a series of constitutional reforms, including the abolition of the Turkish Cypriot veto in the legislature. Turkish opposition to the proposed reforms precipitated new fighting between the Greek and Turkish Cypriot communities. About 200 persons were killed by the time the clashes ebbed Dec. 26. Appeals by the U.S., Britain, Turkey and Greece helped achieve a negotiated truce, and the truce was strengthened by a British-proposed settlement accepted by the warring factions Dec. 30 and 31. Provisions of the settlement included a British-patrolled neutral zone in Nicosia, the free movement of British troops outside the city to prevent further clashes and the exchange of refugees, hostages and prisoners of both sides.

Turks Defy Decree Ending Local Rule

The municipal councils, governing local areas in Cyprus, were officially abolished Jan. 1, 1963. Under a decree issued by Pres. Makarios Dec. 30, 1962, the councils' functions were taken over by the central government through district officers.

But the Turkish Communal Chamber Dec. 31, 1962 had adopted a bill establishing Turkish municipal authorities in Cyprus' 5 principal towns and elsewhere in defiance of the central government. The Turkish chamber asserted that Makarios' abolition of the municipal councils was "unlawful and unconstitutional." The measure adopted by the Turkish chamber was signed by Vice Pres. Fazil Kutchuk. Mayors in Turkish communities agreed at a meeting Dec. 31 to implement the measure. The law was proclaimed in Turkish newspapers Jan. 1. Makarios had forbidden the publication of such statutes in the official government *Gazette* on the ground that the chamber was not empowered to pass municipal legislation.

The ruling Council of Ministers, called into special session by Makarios, further strengthened its move against municipal councils Jan. 3 by enacting a new decree establishing "improvement boards" to control municipal areas where district officers had been appointed to govern. The boards were established under a 1950 Village Law (enacted by the former British colonial government) and invoked by Makarios. The Turks objected to the council's decision on the ground that the Village Law applied only to villages and not to "all former municipal areas" as stated by the new decree.

Turkish leaders Jan. 4 published a "rebel" *Gazette* that carried an order promulgating the municipal-authorities law passed by the Turkish Communal Chamber.

Makarios Plan Provokes Violence

Greek and Turkish Cypriots engaged in armed clashes throughout Cyprus Dec. 21-26, 1963. Turkish Cypriot authorities reported up to 300 persons killed in the communal violence.

The fighting was precipitated by Turkish opposition to 13 constitutional changes proposed by Makarios Nov. 30. The revisions would have outlined more specifically the Turkish minority's constitutional rights but would have abolished its powers to veto laws in the legislature. The Turks had frequently used their veto power because they claimed they had not received all their rights as promised by the 1960 constitution. Contending that the veto impeded effective operation of his government, Makarios often acted without legislative approval.

Among the changes proposed by Makarios: (1) The president and vice president would be denied the right to veto foreign affairs, defense and security decisions made by the House of Representatives or the Council of Ministers; (2) the vice president, a representative of the Turkish minority, would be permitted to "deputize" for the president, a representative of the Greek majority, when the latter was absent or incapacitated; (3) elimination of the required passage by separate majorities of the Greek and Turkish members of the House of Representatives of bills imposing taxes, modifying the electoral law and affecting municipalities (in proposing this amendment, Makarios had charged that the Turkish bloc in the House had used its separate-vote power to defeat a tax bill even though the bloc had not "disagreed with their provisions"); (4) abolition of separate Greek and Turkish courts; (5) abolition of separate municipal Greek and Turkish governments in Cyprus' 5 principal cities.

The first clash occurred Dec. 21 in Nicosia as a Turkish crowd exchanged gunfire with Greek police following an order for a check of identity papers. 2 Turks were killed. The police charged that the Turks had touched off the clash by firing first on the patrol. Turkish leaders declared that the fighting was "a consequence of police methods used against the Turkish community." In a later clash Dec. 21, 2 Turks were wounded as police opened fire on demonstrators in the Turkish sector of Nicosia.

Makarios and Vice Pres. Fazil Kutchuk issued a joint appeal to the Greek and Turkish communities Dec. 21 to remain calm. Acting British High Commissioner Dennis Cleary and U.S. Amb. Fraser Wilkins issued a similar plea Dec. 22 at a meeting with Makarios. The U.S. and British officials expressed "the grave concern of their governments" as the fighting continued. In a message sent to Makarios Dec. 22, the Greek government urged the president to end the communal strife.

The clashes mounted in intensity Dec. 23; 10 persons were killed and the fighting spread from Nicosia to Larnaca.

Britain called on Greece and Turkey Dec. 23 to join London in an appeal to Makarios to end the fighting. Cypriot Foreign Min. Spyros Kyprianou conferred in London Dec. 23 with British Foreign Secy. R. A. Butler and accused the Turkish government of "interference in the internal affairs of Cyprus." Kyprianou said later that Kutchuk had failed to reply to Makarios' proposal to negotiate the constitutional changes and that the Turkish

government rejected the proposed revisions outright. "These proposals were never addressed to the Turkish government,"
Kyprianou complained.

Appeals by the U.S., Britain, Turkey and Greece finally
helped achieve an uneasy cease-fire in the communal clashes.
Diplomatic efforts to end the fighting started Dec. 24. Britain,
Greece and Turkey, as guarantors of Cyprus' independence,
issued a joint appeal to Makarios and other Greek and Turkish
Cypriot leaders to arrange an immediate cease-fire. A British
Foreign Office statement said the 3 governments had "offer[ed]
their joint good offices with a view toward helping resolve the
difficulties which have given rise to the present situation."
Makarios announced Dec. 24 that "British and American independent experts" would help supervise the cease-fire. Makarios
made the announcement after having conferred that day with
Cypriot leaders, U.S. Amb. Wilkins and Acting British High
Commissioner Dennis Cleary. Makarios said later that he had
conferred with Kutchuk and that he and Kutchuk had agreed to
the formation of a Greek-Turkish committee that, "with the
advice of independent [British and American] experts, will insure
observance of a cease-fire and a return to normality."

Greece reported Dec. 25 that Turkey and Britain had
accepted its proposal for placing British, Greek and Turkish
troops in Cyprus (based there by the 1960 independence agreement) under British command to help stop the fighting. The
Greek proposal, which was not fully implemented, followed
reports that Turkey was planning to take military action on its
own in Cyprus to support Turkish Cypriot resistance to the
planned constitutional reforms.

Turkish and Greek troops, ignoring the cease-fire arrangement, moved out of their bases near Nicosia Dec. 25 to participate in the fighting. The entire 600-man Turkish force battled
with Greek Cypriots at Ganili in an effort to relieve beleaguered
Turkish Cypriot irregulars in the city. Another Turkish Cypriot
force fought to break out of a similar Greek Cypriot entrapment
in Nicosia. During the Dec. 25 fighting 3 Turkish jets from
Turkey made low passes over Nicosia but fired no shots. Turkey
also was reported to have sent warships to the vicinity of Cyprus

to bolster its Mediterranean fleet in the area. (Cypriot Defense Min. Osman Orek said Dec. 25 that 100-200 persons had been killed since the fighting started Dec. 21. Kutchuk said Dec. 26 that 300 Cypriots had been slain.)

The communal clashes subsided considerably Dec. 26 as British, Greek and Turkish military commanders met to arrange for establishing cease-fire patrols and for disarming the warring Cypriot factions. In a move to bolster its truce efforts, Britain sent a 750-man battalion from England to Cyprus Dec. 26-27 to reinforce 7,000 British troops stationed there. A British armored squadron of 350 men was flown from Libya to Cyprus Dec. 27.

At separate meetings with Makarios and Kutchuk Dec. 26, Amb. Wilkins handed the 2 leaders identical notes from Pres. Johnson. Mr. Johnson's letters (dated Dec. 25) said: "I cannot believe that you and your fellow-Cypriots will spare any efforts, any sacrifice, to end this terrible fraternal strife." (Wilkins had handed the note to Kutchuk after leading a 9-car convoy into the Turkish sector of Nicosia to rescue 3 Americans and 16 Israelis who had been trapped there by the fighting.) Pres. Johnson Dec. 25 also replied to a letter from Turkish Pres. Cemal Gursel, who had urged the President to end the "dastardly acts of massacres" by Greek "terrorists" in Cyprus. Gursel charged that "atrocities" committed against Turkish women and children bordered on "genocide." Mr. Johnson pledged to support British, Greek and Turkish efforts to bring peace to Cyprus.

Turkish Foreign Min. Feridun Cemal Erkin told the Turkish Senate Dec. 26 that Turkey had accepted the cease-fire on Cyprus. He said the Turkish armed forces had been ordered to refrain from taking any military action in the dispute.

British authorities, unable to get Greek and Turkish military commanders to agree to a 3-nation truce patrol, began their own cease-fire observation patrols Dec. 27 There was a halt in the fighting that day except for a brief exchange of gunfire between Greek and Turkish Cypricts in Nicosia. But sporadic firing continued through Dec. 29. The regular Turkish troops that had left their barracks Dec. 25 took complete control of key roads in the Nicosia area. Greek troops that had left their Cyprus compound that day also were dug in at strategic points around the city.

British Plan Eases Tensions

British Commonwealth Relations Secy. Duncan Sandys arrived in Nicosia Dec. 28, 1963 and won agreement Dec. 30 and 31 to the first of several steps he had proposed for easing tensions. Sandys conferred with Makarios and Kutchuk Dec. 28 and 29. Sandys said after the Dec. 29 talks that he had proposed a peace plan that called for: (a) the establishing of a British-patrolled neutral zone in Nicosia to separate the Greek and Turkish Cypriots; (b) the free movement of British patrols in areas outside Nicosia; (c) arrangements for the removal of Turkish dead and wounded from Greek-held Omorphita, near Nicosia; (d) the exchange of refugees, hostages and other prisoners of both sides. Sandys appealed to the Greek Cypriots to permit the restoration of phone and postal services in the Turkish communities and the resumption of Turkish-language broadcasts.

Greek and Turkish Cypriot leaders Dec. 30 signed an agreement creating the Nicosia neutral zone. British troops immediately were moved into the cease-fire line that separated the Turkish Cypriots (in the northern part of the city) from the Greek Cypriots (in the southern part). Both sides also granted British troops permission to move freely in Nicosia and in other parts of Cyprus.

Sandys' proposal for the exchange of prisoners was accepted and implemented Dec. 31. Greek Cypriots released 470 Turkish Cypriots held in a Nicosia school, 76 captives from a Nicosia prison and 15 held in Kyrenia, a city on the northern coast. The Turks released 26 Greek Cypriots held in private homes in Nicosia.

Despite the successful efforts to reduce the danger of further fighting, the irreconcilable views of the Greek and Turkish Cypriot communities remained apparent in statements delivered Dec. 30 by Kutchuk and Makarios. Kutchuk declared that "the Cyprus constitution is dead" because there was "no possibility" that Greek and Turkish Cypriots could live together. When questioned by newsmen as to whether his statement meant he favored partition of the island, Kutchuk replied: "Call it partition if you like." Makarios said that he would seek to abolish the treaties under which Britain, Greece and Turkey guaranteed the constitution and the territorial integrity of Cyprus. Makarios said "the root of the tragic events is found in our constitution and in a general way, in the Zurich and London agreements."

UN Takes Up Charge of Turkish Intervention

The UN Security Council met in emergency session in New York Dec. 27-28, 1963 to consider a complaint that Turkey had intervened in Cyprus' internal affairs "by the threat and use of force." The charge and request for the meeting had been made Dec. 26 and 27 by Zenon G. Rossides, Cyprus' delegate to the UN. In a letter to U.S. Amb.-to-UN Adlai Stevenson, Council president for December, Rossides had said that the Turkish Cypriots had started the communal unrest and that Turkey had committed an "act of aggression" by interfering in the disorders.

Rossides' first request for a UN meeting had dealt with only the fighting on Cyprus. His 2d appeal for an immediate Council meeting was based on what he described as his government's reports of Turkish naval movements off Cyprus. He said the force consisted of 4 destroyers, 5 submarines and 3 other ships believed to be troop transports. (Greek Foreign Min. Sophocles Venizelos conferred in Athens Dec. 28 with the U.S. and British ambassadors and voiced concern over the reported Turkish naval movement. A Turkish note sent to Greece Dec. 27 had said that the Turkish ships were on maneuvers that had originally been scheduled for November.) Turkish delegate Adnan Kural had said the Turkish ships were not threatening Cyprus but were merely moving from one port to another.

The Council adjourned early Dec. 28 without taking action. Acting Council Pres. Francis T. P. Plimpton said Council members would confer on when the Cyprus matter should be taken up again.

In a letter delivered to Stevenson Dec. 28, Rossides charged that "3 Turkish military jet planes again violated Cyprus airspace by flying low ... over Nicosia." Kutchuk charged in a letter to UN Secy. Gen. U Thant Dec. 30 that Rossides' appeal to the

UN Security Council was "illegal and unconstitutional" because Makarios had submitted the appeal to the Council without authorization of his ministers.

STRIFE & UN PEACE ROLE JAN.-JULY 1964

The constitutional dispute remained unresolved at the start of 1964 and led to a fresh upsurge of communal fighting. The clashes mounted in intensity, threatening to plunge Cyprus into full-scale warfare. Faced with this peril, international leaders spurred efforts to end the fighting. The first such attempt was made jointly by Britain and the U.S. They advanced a plan for a 10,000-man NATO force to assure observance of the cease-fire negotiated in 1963; UN representatives had already arrived in Cyprus to observe that truce. The Anglo-American proposal was submitted following a breakdown of a multilateral conference aimed at resolving the differences between the Greek and Turkish Cypriots.

Pres. Makarios objected to the peace-force plan and opposed a follow-up U.S.-British proposal of a UN "link" with the NATO contingent. The impasse prompted Britain and Cyprus to submit the dispute to the UN Security Council, which approved the establishment of a UN peace-keeping force. The resolution also provided for a UN mediator to seek a permanent political settlement. The first UN troops landed on the island Mar. 14, and the UN Force in Cyprus (UNFICYP) became operational.

The arrival of the UN contingent caused Turkey to call off a threatened invasion of Cyprus. Ankara had warned that it would send troops to Cyprus to aid outnumbered Turkish Cypriots then under heavy attack by Greek Cypriots.

Cyprus faced another political crisis in April when Makarios abrogated the 1960 Treaty of Alliance. This action led to another outbreak of clashes between Greek and Turkish Cypriots. The fighting culminated in a massive, but unsuccessful attack on St. Hilarion Castle, the last major Turkish Cypriot stronghold in northeastern Cyprus. A cease-fire ordered by Makarios ended the fighting Apr. 29. In the wake of this communal battling, fresh international appeals were issued to all sides in the dispute to help bring peace to the island. UN Secy. Gen. U Thant proposed a new peace formula, and Pres. Johnson held mediative discussions

*with Turkish Premier Ismet Inonu and Greek Premier George
Papandreou. The meeting with Inonu followed a warning issued
to the Turkish leader by Mr. Johnson not to invade Cyprus.*

*Meanwhile, EOKA leader George Grivas ended his 5 years
of exile from Cyprus. Returning to the island, he proclaimed that
he came back to help restore peace.*

Truce Violations; UN Observers Arrive

The cease-fire that had been negotiated Dec. 24, 1963 continued in a precarious state at the start of 1964. Turkish Cypriots
Jan. 1 attacked a Greek Orthodox monastery at Glaktrofousa,
killed 2 monks and a 14-year-old novice and wounded 3 monks.
Turkish Cypriot homes in Nicosia had been set afire Dec. 31,
1963 and Jan. 1. It was reported Jan. 3 that more than 30 homes
had been set ablaze in the Nicosia suburb of Omorphita.

The U.S. embassy in Nicosia was bombed Feb. 4. The
evacuation from Cyprus of dependents of U.S. government
officials began the next day, when American women and children
were flown to Beirut, Lebanon. (The transfer of 750 U.S.
dependents was completed Feb. 13.) The bombing led to a U.S.
decision to halt operations in Cyprus of U.S. aid missions and the
U.S. Information Agency. No one was injured in the embassy
blast, but 3 rooms were badly damaged. U.S. Amb. Fraser
Wilkins, in a personal protest to Makarios Feb. 4, said he had "no
confidence" in the ability of the Cyprus police to protect Americans; Wilkins then authorized the evacuation of the U.S.
nationals. Makarios assailed the bombing as "a crime of the most
revolting nature." The bombing took place at a time when strong
anti-American feelings were being expressed in reaction to the
U.S. support of the NATO-peace force proposal for Cyprus.
Wilkins charged Feb. 5 that the Cypriot press was conducting an
"organized campaign" against the U.S.

Britain Jan. 3 had completed airlifting the last of 2,000 troop
reinforcements for its Cyprus garrison. The British patrol force
expanded its truce-supervising activities Jan. 5 as a regiment of
Royal Air Force soldiers moved from Nicosia into nearby Trak-

homas and Omorphita. British High Commissioner Sir Arthur Clark Jan. 7 announced Greek and Turkish Cypriot agreement to the removal of roadblocks and armed posts in Nicosia and in other centers. The agreement followed 2 days of talks by a political liaison committee composed of Clark, the Greek and Turkish ambassadors and Greek and Turkish Cypriot leaders. Exceptions to the agreement were in the Lefka and Xeros area in the northwest. The committee had been unable to make any contact with that sector, where an estimated 6,000 Turkish Cypriots were besieged in their dug-in positions by a larger Greek Cypriot force.

UN and Cypriot authorities agreed in New York Jan. 16 to the stationing of a UN official in Cyprus to observe the ceasefire. Britain, Turkey and Greece had urged UN Secy. Gen. U Thant Jan. 3 to appoint such an observer. Thant assigned the observer post to Lt. Gen. Prem Singh Gyani of India, who had commanded the UN Emergency Force in Gaza. Gyani said on arriving in Cyprus Jan. 17 that he expected to remain until the end of February and then report to Thant. Cypriot Representative to UN Rossides had told Thant in New York Jan. 6 that his government approved in principle the stationing of a UN observer in Cyprus, but the Cyprus government barred Gyani from receiving petitions or complaints from individual Cypriots.

U.S. & Britain Propose NATO Force

The creation of a NATO force of at least 10,000 troops (including American soldiers) to maintain peace between the Greek and Turkish communities of Cyprus was proposed jointly by Britain and the U.S. Jan. 31, 1964. Greece immediately accepted the plan. Cypriot Pres. Makarios gave conditional approval Feb. 1. *The text of the Anglo-American proposal:*

"(1) For reasons which have been explained, it is proposed that a peace-keeping force shall be established in Cyprus drawn from NATO countries. Such a force shall remain in Cyprus for the shortest possible period necessary to accomplish its mission. The countries concerned shall commit themselves to retain in Cyprus forces which they contribute for a period of not more than 3 months.

"(2) The governments of Greece and Turkey undertake not to exercise their right of unilateral intervention under Article 3 of the Treaty of Guarantee for 3 months on the understanding that the peace-keeping force will be in place during this period.

"(3) Parties concerned agree to accept mediation of their differences in the spirit of mutual accommodation and to the appointment of a mediator from a NATO country other than one of the 3 guarantor powers.

"(4) The force shall be drawn from such NATO countries as wish to participate, but its establishment and operation will not be under NATO control.

"(5) The force will augment the British force engaged in keeping the peace on the island in accordance with a proposal of the guarantor powers accepted by Pres. Makarios and Vice Pres. Kutchuk on Dec. 26 [1963]. The force will be under British command. The commander of the force will receive political guidance from an intergovernmental committee of representatives of the participating countries sitting in London.

"(6) The total force must be adequate for the mission for which it is conceived and not less than 10,000 men.

"(7) Greek and Turkish contingents now on the island shall be part of the force. Neither contingent shall be augmented.

"(8) The precise definition of the task and status of the force will be subject to further discussions."

(France Feb. 5 rejected participation in the proposed force. Information Min. Alain Peyrefitte said France could not join a Cyprus patrol because Paris had not taken part in the drafting of the 1959 treaty that had ended the fighting between the Greek and Turkish Cypriots.)

The NATO-force proposal was originated by Britain after it appeared that a multilateral conference in London, in progress since Jan. 15, faced an impasse in its efforts to settle the differences between the Greek and Turkish communities. The London meeting was presided over by British Commonwealth Secy. Duncan Sandys and was attended by delegations representing Greece and Turkey and the Greek and Turkish Cypriot communities. Delegation chiefs: Greek Foreign Min. Christos X. Palamas; Turkish Foreign Min. Feridun Cemal Erkin; Cyprus Foreign Min. Spyros Achilles Kyprianou, a Greek; Cyprus Defense Min. Osman Orek, a Turk.

The London deadlock developed over these opposing viewpoints: The Turkish Cypriots, fearful of their minority status, insisted on the partition of Cyprus and self-administration of their own section; the Greek Cypriot position, as stated by Kyprianou, called for "a completely independent state of Cyprus in which the [Greek] majority should rule and the rights of the [Turkish] minority would be safeguarded."

The NATO-force proposal submitted at the London con-
ference was first made public Jan. 26 when it was reported in
London that Britain had appealed to the U.S., France, Italy and
West Germany to contribute troops for such a force in Cyprus.
Britain had argued that (a) its military commitments in Malaysia
and east Africa made it difficult to maintain the British force in
Cyprus without outside assistance and (b) Cyprus actually was a
NATO problem because the dispute could bring Turkey and
Greece, both NATO members, into military conflict with each
other. The U.S., at first reluctant to join a Cyprus peace force,
finally agreed after the acceptance of these 2 principal American
demands: (1) Cyprus government approval of the NATO force
and (2) agreement by Britain, Greece and Turkey to a 3-month
suspension of their right to intervene militarily in Cyprus.

U.S. opposition to the NATO-force plan had been overcome
in talks held in London Jan. 26-27 by U.S. Atty. Gen. Robert F.
Kennedy with Prime Min. Sir Alec Douglas-Home. Final U.S.
agreement was reached following consultations held in Washington Jan. 28 by a British mission, headed by Lt. Gen. Geoffrey H.
Baker, vice chief of the General Staff, with U.S. Defense and
State Department officials.

Makarios had announced outright rejection of the peace-
force plan Feb. 1. But he reversed this stand after formally
receiving the plan Feb. 2 from British State Undersecy. for
Commonwealth Relations Cyril C. Pickard and U.S. Amb.
Wilkins. Makarios' reply was made to the London conference
through Foreign Min. Kyprianou. In it, Makarios accepted in
principle the idea of the NATO peace force but said he regarded
some proposals unacceptable or in need of clarification. In submitting Makarios' answer, Kyprianou reiterated the previous
demands he had made at the conference that Greek and Turkish
troops should be barred from any peace-keeping operation in
Cyprus. Kyprianou was particularly concerned about the presence of Turkish troops. He also demanded a guarantee that the
NATO force protect Cyprus from outside attack. Kyprianou
said a precondition of Makarios' acceptance of more foreign
troops in Cyprus was submission of greater details on this aspect
of the forces' function. Kyprianou expressed concern that the

NATO units, unguided by detailed rules of operation, would be in no position to prevent Turkish troops from shielding a Turkish Cypriot population shift that might pave the way for the eventual establishment of *de facto* partition of the island. Kyprianou argued for a peace force that would be under the jurisdiction of the UN Security Council, which he felt would allay the Cyprus government's anxiety over Turkey's intentions toward Cyprus. Britain, the U.S. and Turkey opposed a Security Council role on the ground that it would bring the Soviet Union into the controversy and possibly create greater tensions between Greece and Turkey.

Questioning the advisability of appointing a NATO political adviser, Kyprianou argued that Cyprus would be more interested in mediation if Britain, Greece and Turkey agreed to discuss ending the 1960 treaty that permitted them to intervene in Cyprus.

The London conference had been agreed to by Greek and Turkish Cypriot leaders Jan. 2 after details had been worked out by Sandys during his negotiations with all sides in the controversy. Sandys, who had been in Cyprus since Dec. 28, 1963 on a peace mission, left for London Jan. 2 after completing arrangements for the conference.

Makarios had declared Jan. 2 that, as a delegate to the London talks, he would seek the abrogation of the treaties that bound Cyprus to Greece, Turkey and Britain. Denouncing the provisions of the pact that permitted Britain, Turkey and Greece to station troops in Cyprus to guarantee its independence, Makarios said that abolishing the treaties would help "create a really independent and unified state free of any form of outside interference and intervention." Makarios also said he would oppose the partition of Cyprus as advocated by Turkish Cypriots. In telegrams sent to world leaders Jan. 1, Makarios had announced his intention to seek an end to the treaties. Makarios also had charged that regular Turkish troops, who had left their base near Nicosia Dec. 25, 1962 to participate in the communal fighting, were still occupying strategic positions in violation, of Cyprus' territorial integrity.

Turkish Foreign Min. Erkin said Jan. 2 that Turkey opposed Makarios' plan to abrogate Cyprus' treaties. Instead, Erkin called for "strengthen[ing] the guarantees for the security of the Turkish community on the island, which recent events have plainly proved to be inadequate." Erkin said he had proposed to Britain and Greece the expansion of the Greek and Turkish garrison on Cyprus.

Greece rejected Erkin's proposal later Jan. 2 and submitted the entire Cyprus dispute that day to the NATO Council in Paris. The Council heard separate British, Greek and Turkish reports.

In a pre-London conference statement, Cypriot Vice Pres. Fazil Kutchuk said Jan. 3 that partition of Cyprus was the only way to "save humanity and the world from continuous trouble" and to guarantee the "Turkish Cypriots their minority rights."

Zenon G. Rossides, Cyprus' chief delegate to the UN, warned in New York Jan. 6 that partition was not "debatable" and that if the matter were brought up at the London conference the talks would come to "an abrupt end." Rossides said that the Cyprus constitution did not permit partition and that the Turkish minority had more rights than any other minority in the world.

New U.S.-British Plan

A new Anglo-U.S. plan for an international military force in Cyprus would have provided a UN "link" with the projected 10,000-man NATO army proposed for policing the truce between the island's warring Greek and Turkish communities. The plan was made public Feb. 6 after it had already been rejected by Makarios Feb. 3. The plan proposed that the UN get reports on the force but not have an actual voice in its operations. The plan was designed to overcome the objections of Makarios, who had insisted that any outside force on Cyprus be under the authority of the UN Security Council. Makarios had rejected the original Anglo-U.S. plan because it made no such provision.

The U.S. and Britain were reported Feb. 9 to have further modified their proposal in an effort to overcome objections of all parties. The modified plan provided for: (a) the inclusion in the force of soldiers from European countries outside NATO; (b) participation in the international force by Greek and Turkish troops regularly stationed in Cyprus; (c) attendance by a Cypriot government representative at the meetings of the political committee that was to advise the force's British commander.

Greece accepted the modified proposal but only on condition that it be approved by the Cypriot government. Turkey also gave conditional approval Feb. 9. Ankara insisted that the force's principal function be confined to maintaining security on Cyprus pending a political settlement. Turkey opposed Makarios' demand that the peace force maintain the island's unity.

Cypriot Foreign Min. Kyprianou rejected the Anglo-U.S. troop plan outright as it was presented to him in London Feb. 10 by British Commonwealth Relations Secy. Sandys. Kyprianou reiterated previous Cypriot government demands that the force be answerable to the UN Security Council. (British Prime Min. Sir Alec Douglas-Home Feb. 9 had questioned the feasibility of linking the proposed peace force to the UN Security Council. He said: "That is a lot more difficult for us and for other countries as well. It could mean that Russia could veto and interfere in any number of ways.")

U.S. State Undersecy. George Ball, representing Pres. Johnson, had flown from Washington Feb. 8 to visit the principals in the Cyprus dispute to press for acceptance of the proposed international force. Ball arrived in London Feb. 9 and conferred with British officials and later with Kyprianou. Ball conferred with Greek officials in Athens Feb. 10 and with Turkish leaders in Ankara Feb 11. He then went to Nicosia Feb. 12 to see Makarios.

Makarios met with Ball and British State Undersecy. for Commonwealth Relations Cyril Pickard in Nicosia Feb. 12-14 and rejected the Anglo-U.S. proposal. In formally spurning the plan, Makarios said Feb. 13 that "if these proposals were accepted the situation would be more complicated." Insisting on his previous demands that the composition of the proposed force and its functions be approved in advance, Makarios said: "When this is agreed upon, then we can discuss whether the force will be under full control of the [UN] Security Council or just linked with it." Offering a counter-proposal Makarios said he would prefer a peace-keeping force composed of British Commonwealth soldiers rather than the NATO units proposed by Britain and the U.S. Makarios warned in a broadcast Feb. 16 that Cyprus' "territorial integrity, security and peace are under serious threat." The country's "2 great dangers," he said, were "the danger of foreign intervention and the danger of resumption of internal disturbances on a large scale." Makarios said no international peace-keeping force on Cyprus could accomplish its mission "if the Greeks and Turks of Cyprus do not show goodwill and a desire to live together in peace. . . .'

Ball returned to Washington Feb. 16 after reporting on his negotiations with Makarios to Greek, Turkish and British officials in their respective capitals Feb. 14-16. Ball reported to Pres. Johnson Feb. 17 and said later that the President had agreed with him that (a) "we are faced with a situation of considerable gravity" and (b) it was "imperative that we take the necessary measures to restore peace and order" in Cyprus.

British Foreign Secy. R. A. Butler had discussed the Anglo-U.S. proposal with UN Secy. Gen. U Thant at UN headquarters in New York Feb. 11.

USSR Warns Against Western Intervention

The Soviet Union warned Feb. 7, 1964 that it would not tolerate intervention by the Western powers in the Cyprus situation. It charged that the proposals for the establishment of a joint peace-keeping force were motivated by a single aim: "actual occupation by the armed forces of NATO" in order to "place this small neutral state under NATO's military control." The Soviet warning was delivered in parallel notes sent by Premier Nikita S. Khrushchev to Pres. Johnson, Pres. Makarios, British Prime Min. Douglas-Home, French Pres. de Gaulle, Greek Premier John Paraskevopoulos and Turkish Premier Ismet Inonu.

Khrushchev charged that traditional differences between Greek and Turkish Cypriots had been "whipped up from the outside" to provide a pretext for foreign intervention in the island's affairs. The notes expressed full support for the Makarios government and its efforts to settle the island's unrest; they charged that the NATO powers had sabotaged Makarios' peace efforts and were attempting to prevent a new Cypriot appeal for discussion of the island's problems by the UN Security Council. The West's intent, Khrushchev charged, was to prove that "a solution of these internal problems can be brought to Cyprus only by foreign bayonets." He warned that the Soviet government "cannot remain indifferent to the situation that is taking shape in the . . . Eastern Mediterranean . . . not very distant from the southern frontiers of the USSR."

British Prime Min. Douglas-Home Feb. 8 rejected Khrushchev's views as "offensive" and "unfounded." In a note to Khrushchev, Douglas-Home declared that the Soviet government's communication was "completely divorced from reality" and intended to increase tensions on the island. Douglas-Home made it clear that he resented Khrushchev's charge that Britain's intervention had been designed to subject the island to NATO domination. He asserted that Britain had sent troops to Cyprus only at the request of the Makarios government and only "to help to maintain peace and security in the island."

Pres. Johnson said in a note sent to Khrushchev Mar. 4 (made public Mar. 6) that the premier's "message was based upon a seriously mistaken appreciation both of the situation in Cyprus and of the aims of the U.S. in agreeing to lend its assistance in improving this situation." Mr. Johnson assured Khrushchev that the U.S. had "been cooperating with the governments concerned, including . . . Cyprus, for one purpose alone, that of assisting the Cypriots to restore a peaceful situation in Cyprus." Mr. Johnson said he hoped the USSR would join the U.S. and other nations and "strive not to inflame passions from without."

UN Votes to Send Peace Force

Following Makarios' rejection of the new Anglo-U.S. proposal for an international military force, Britain and Cyprus Feb. 15, 1964 requested an emergency meeting of the UN Security Council to explore the matter further. The Council opened debate Feb. 18 and voted Mar. 4 to create a multi-nation UN force to keep the peace in Cyprus.

Britain's request for a Security Council meeting represented a reversal of London policy in the Cyprus dispute. Britain had been wary of Council intervention lest the Soviet Union use its power of veto in the Security Council to block any peace moves. In a letter to Council Pres. Carlos Alfredo Bernardes of Brazil, British delegate Sir Patrick Dean requested that the Council take up the issue. Dean said in his letter that "while agreement on these arrangements [for a peace-keeping force in Cyprus] has been reached among the guarantor powers [Britain, Greece and Turkey] and certain other governments, I regret to inform you that owing to the inability so far of the Cyprus government to agree, it has not yet proved possible to bring arrangements contemplated into effect."

The U.S., which also had opposed a Council session, changed its position and said in a statement through Amb. Adlai E. Stevenson that Britain had asked for the meeting "after full consultation with the U.S."

Cypriot delegate Zenon Rossides, in his Feb. 15 request for a Council meeting, warned that Cyprus faced an imminent invasion by Turkey. (Ankara was reported Feb. 15 to have informed Britain and the U.S. that it would not intervene in Cyprus while peace efforts were in progress. The Turks, however, were said to have warned that they would invade if heavy fighting between Greek and Turkish Cypriots were renewed.)

A starting point for debate was provided by Secy. Gen. U Thant in a plan he submitted Feb. 15 to Britain, Turkey, Greece, Cyprus and the U.S. Its principal points: (1) An international peace-keeping force should be formed with the consent of the 4 principal parties without formal Council authorization. (2) On agreement, the secretary general would report the force's formation to the Security Council; the Council would then adopt a resolution taking note of the 4-power agreement. (3) If Britain,

Turkey, Greece and Cyprus failed to agree on a peace force, a mediator would be appointed to seek a solution within 2 weeks. (4) The secretary general or the Council president would issue a statement upholding Cyprus' independence and territorial integrity; such a statement would be aimed at satisfying Cyprus Pres. Makarios' repeated demands for a Council guarantee of his country's freedom.

Cypriot Foreign Min. Kyprianou rejected the secretary general's proposal in talks with Thant Feb. 18. Kyprianou insisted that his government would accept nothing short of an outright Council guarantee of Cyprus' territorial integrity.

At a meeting with Thant Feb. 18, Turkish Amb.-to-U.S. Turgut Menemencioglu expressed his government's opposition to a Council commitment on Cyprus. Menemencioglu said Ankara sought a Council resolution that would specifically indorse Cyprus' constitution and the 1960 treaty that guaranteed its independence.

Kyprianou reiterated his stand as Council debate started later Feb. 18. He said a Council guarantee on Cyprus would be "the greatest contribution toward keeping peace" on the island. Kyprianou read parts of what he called a Turkish document that suggested provoking Greek-Turkish Cypriot clashes as a pretext for Turkish intervention and annexation of Cyprus. Menemencioglu called Kyprianou's accusation "distorted." He countercharged that "Greek Cypriot terrorists" were planning a "hideous massacre" of Turkish Cypriots.

British delegate Dean urged the Council Feb. 18 to indorse Thant's Feb. 15 appeal to all sides in the Cyprus dispute to practice restraint. Dean also asked the Council: (a) to urge all parties in the controversy to confer with Thant "to secure the establishment of an effective peace-keeping force as soon as possible"; (b) to appoint "an impartial mediator" to help work out a peace settlement; (c) to call on all countries concerned to respect Cyprus' security "in accordance with the treaty of guarantee."

U.S. Amb. Stevenson, in Council debate Feb. 19, called for quick agreement to a peace force. Stevenson denied a charge by Soviet delegate Nikolai T. Fedorenko that the proposed Anglo-U.S. plan for a NATO troop force on Cyprus was actually a "plot" to establish a "military bridgehead" in Cyprus. Stevenson said no country would serve in the force without the Cypriot government's consent. Although the U.S. would be willing to be represented in the peace force if requested by Britain, Greece, Turkey and Cyprus, it would be "delighted" not to, Stevenson declared.

British delegate Dean Feb. 19 disputed Fedorenko's charge that Dean had failed to deny in Feb. 18 debate that Britain planned to commit "aggression" in Cyprus. Dean said that the British security force had not inflicted any casualties on Greek or Turkish Cypriots and that the situation there would have been "infinitely worse" without the British troops.

(In his speech Feb. 19, Fedorenko also supported Cyprus' demands for a Security Council resolution guaranteeing Cyprus' independence.)

Thant reported to the Security Council Feb. 25 that an "impasse" had been reached in his efforts to establish a peace-keeping force. Thant, who, since Feb. 20, had been conferring on his proposal with the principal parties in the dispute, said the "position[s] on certain key issues have been firmly taken and maintained" during his talks with Turkish and Cypriot officials. The deadlock in the negotiations developed over the issue of the 1960 treaty guaranteeing Cyprus' independence. In his talks with Thant, Kyprianou, reflecting his government's fear of Turkish intervention, had insisted that the Security Council adopt a resolution guaranteeing Cyprus' independence and that no mention be made of the 1960 treaty. British and U.S. officials had contended in their discussions with Thant that acceptance of the Cypriot position would serve to abrogate the 1960 treaty and that the Council was not authorized to take such a step. Turkey also had supported the maintenance of the 1960 treaty on the ground that it would permit it to send troops to Cyprus to protect the Turkish minority.

The burden of finding a solution to the dispute was passed on Feb. 25 to the 6 elected members of the Security Council: Bolivia, Brazil, Czechoslovakia, the Ivory Coast, Morocco and Norway.

In Council debate Feb. 25 Norwegian delegate Sivert A. Nielsen urged acceptance of Thant's peace-force plan because, he said, it would "remove the distrust ... now prevailing between the parties." Moroccan delegate Dey Ould Sidi Baba called for amending the Cypriot constitution to "give the necessary guarantees to the Turkish minority." Czech delegate Jiri Hajek supported the Cypriot government position by urging the Council to "reaffirm the independence, sovereignty and territorial integrity of Cyprus."

The Security Council Mar. 4 unanimously approved a resolution providing for an international peace-keeping force in Cyprus for a 3-month period. The resolution also provided for the appointment of a mediator to seek a political solution to the dispute between the island's Greek and Turkish communities. The proposal was accepted by Greece, Turkey and the Greek and Turkish Cypriots. The resolution, similar to the plan proposed by Thant, had been drafted and introduced Mar. 2 by 5 of the 6 non-permanent Council members (Bolivia, Brazil, the Ivory Coast, Morocco and Norway).

The resolution assigned to Thant the tasks of appointing the mediator and the commander of the force and of recruiting the force. The force's size was to be determined "in consultations with" Cyprus, Greece, Turkey and Britain. (Thant formally asked Brazil, Canada, Finland, Ireland and Sweden to provide the soldiers.) The force commander was to report to Thant, who in turn was to keep the Council fully informed of its activities. The force's operations were to be financed by the contributing nations and the government of Cyprus. The mediator and his staff were to be paid through UN funds.

Text of the UN resolution:

"Noting that the present situation with regard to Cyprus is likely to threaten international peace and security and may further deteriorate unless additional measures are promptly taken to maintain peace and to seek out a durable solution;

"Considering the positions taken by the parties in relation to the treaties signed at Nicosia on Aug. 16, 1960;

"Having in mind the relevant provisions of the UN Charter and its Article 2 Paragraph 4, which reads: 'All members shall refrain in their international relations from the threat or use of force against the territorial integrity or political independence of any state, or in any other manner inconsistent with the purposes of the United Nations':

"(1) Calls upon all member-states, in conformity with their obligations under the UN Charter, to refrain from any action or threat of action likely to worsen the situation in the sovereign Republic of Cyprus, or to endanger international peace;

"(2) Asks the government of Cyprus, which has the responsibility for the maintenance and restoration of law and order, to take all additional measures necessary to stop violence and bloodshed in Cyprus;

"(3) Calls upon the communities in Cyprus and their leaders to act with the utmost restraint;

"(4) Recommends the creation, with the consent of the government of Cyprus, of a UN peace-keeping force in Cyprus. The composition and size of the force shall be established by the [UN] secretary general, in consultation with the governments of Cyprus, Greece, Turkey and the United Kingdom. The commander of the force shall be appointed by the secretary general and report to him. The secretary general, who shall keep the governments providing the force fully informed, shall report periodically to the Security Council on its operation;

"(5) Recommends that the function of the force should be, in the interest of preserving international peace and security, to use its best efforts to prevent a recurrence of fighting and, as necessary, to contribute to the maintenance and restoration of law and order and a return to normal conditions;

"(6) Recommends that the stationing of the force shall be for a period of 3 months, all costs pertaining to it being met, in a manner to be agreed upon by them, by the governments providing the contingents and by the government of Cyprus. The secretary general may also accept voluntary contributions for that purpose;

"(7) Recommends further that the secretary general designate, in agreement with the government of Cyprus and the governments of Greece, Turkey and the United Kingdom, a mediator, who shall use his best endeavors with the representatives of the communities and also with the aforesaid 4 governments, for the purpose of promoting a peaceful solution and an agreed settlement of the problem confronting Cyprus, in accordance with the UN Charter, having in mind the well-being of the people of Cyprus as a whole and the preservation of international peace and security. The mediator shall report periodically to the secretary general on his efforts;

"(8) Requests the secretary general to provide, from funds of the United Nations, as appropriate, for the remuneration and expenses of the mediator and his staff."

Although voting for the resolution, France, the USSR and Czechoslovakia had objected in principle to granting Thant control over the Cyprus force. Cypriot Foreign Min. Kyprianou said the resolution was "a victory for all the people of Cyprus" because it protected them against foreign interference. Pres. Johnson hailed the resolution as "a major step towards peace." Pres. Makarios said the resolution meant that "Turkey cannot in

the future threaten intervention in Cyprus, invoking the treaty of
guarantee." A spokesman for Cyprus Vice Pres. Fazil Kutchuk
interpreted the resolution as meaning "that the Greek [Cypriot]
attempt to abrogate the treaty of guarantee has been rejected."

Thant's appointment of Jose Rolz-Bennett of Guatemala as
the UN mediator of the Cyprus dispute was rejected by Turkey
Mar. 8. Foreign Min. Cemal Feridun Erkin said Ankara felt that
Rolz-Bennett did not have "the qualifications to fulfill such a difficult task." Thant received official notification of Turkey's
rejection Mar. 12. Britain, Greece and Cyprus had approved
Rolz-Bennett's appointment.

Greeks Demonstrate Against U.S. & Britain

While the UN Security Council labored to solve the crisis in
Cyprus, anti-U.S. and anti-British demonstrations were staged in
Greece in protest against alleged U.S. and British bias in favor of
the Turkish Cypriots.

In a protest to U.S. Amb. Henry R. Labouisse Feb. 29,
Greek Premier George Papandreou specifically cited speeches by
U.S. officials, particularly those made by U.S. Amb. Stevenson
in UN Security Council debate, as objectionable to Greece and
the Greek Cypriots. In a nationwide broadcast Feb. 29,
Papandreou called for revision of Cyprus treaties of guarantee,
which the U.S. and Britain had upheld in Council debate.
Papandreou said the current Cyprus crisis was "a tragic result"
of those "inapplicable" agreements. Papandreou had sent Pres.
Johnson a message (published Feb. 29) in which he said Greece
hoped that the U.S. would retain its traditional "aversion for any
form of expediency in international life...in resolving the
problems confronting us."

The Greek government Feb. 29 banned a rebroadcast over
Athens radio of U.S., British and French press comments on
Cyprus on the ground that they were "hostile to the Greek case."

3,000 Greek students, carrying pro-Greek Cypriot placards,
demonstrated before the U.S. embassy in Athens Feb. 29. Some
demonstrators handed an embassy official a resolution
demanding self-determination for Cyprus. After burning an

effigy of Pres. Johnson, the demonstrators marched to the British embassy, staged a similar demonstration there and delivered a copy of the resolution. The U.S. embassy was the scene of another protest Mar. 3, when several thousand persons massed there and shouted anti-American slogans. The demonstrators burned 2 pictures of Pres. Johnson. Anti-U.S. mobs Mar. 3 also marched on U.S. Information Service (USIS) headquarters on the Greek island of Rhodes and smashed the building's windows. Papandreou later Mar. 3 directed police authorities to protect all foreign embassies but specifically permitted demonstrations "in favor of the just struggle of Cypriot Hellenism."

Following UN approval of the Cyprus peace-keeping resolution, Athens demonstrators Mar. 4 again rallied before the U.S. and British embassies. As a result of the continued rioting, the USIS announced Mar. 4 that the scheduled Mar. 5 visit to Greece of units of the U.S. 6th Fleet has been "temporarily postponed at the suggestion of the Greek government." The proposed fleet visit had been protested at a rally at Salonika, where 30,000 persons turned out to hear speeches denouncing the U.S. and Britain for their "anti-Greek bias" in the Cyprus dispute.

Fighting Accelerates

While international efforts were being pressed for a peaceful solution of the Cyprus question, fighting on the island increased in intensity in February-March 1964. At least 12 persons were killed and more than 30 wounded Feb. 6 in a gun battle at Ayia Sozomenos, 16 miles from Nicosia, and at least 50 Cypriots were killed and 100 wounded in a series of Greek-Turkish clashes that raged throughout Limassol Feb. 11-13; the Limassol fighting eventually ceased after a British security force arranged a truce.

Britain began to fly reinforcements to Cyprus as the increased fighting strained the ability of British security forces to maintain peace. 500 British soldiers were flown to Cyprus from Malta Feb. 8. The transfer from England to Cyprus of 170 men of the 3d Division's headquarters staff was completed Feb. 13. Another 1,500 troops, including armored cars, began to leave

England for Cyprus Feb. 20. Pres. Makarios Feb. 21 expressed opposition to the expansion of the British security force. Noting that reinforcements had raised the number of the British security patrol to 7,000 men, Makarios said "there is no room left for a further increase in military forces in the island."

(1,200 British women and children were ordered evacuated from Cyprus for security reasons. The first planeload was flown to Britain Feb. 19. British families were reported Feb. 13 to have been evacuated from Limassol to the British base at Episkopi.)

British Commonwealth Relations Secy. Duncan Sandys told the British House of Commons Feb. 17 that he had protested the previous day to Cypriot Foreign Min. Kyprianou that Britain "had ample information" that arms were being smuggled into Cyprus "with the full knowledge and approval of the Cyprus government." According to diplomatic sources, the arms were being shipped to Greek Cypriots from Greece and the United Arab Republic. The weapons from Greece were said to come mainly from businessmen who supported the union of Cyprus with Greece.

In the wake of the increased fighting, Makarios Feb. 25 announced government approval of a plan to increase Cyprus' legal security force of 1,500-2,000 policemen and gendarmerie to 7,000 men. Makarios said the expansion was needed to cope with "the abnormal situation" on Cyprus. Makarios also said that orders had been issued to "disarm all citizens unlawfully carrying arms." This order apparently applied to the 23,000 armed Greek Cypriots who heretofore had been regarded as "legal forces of the republic." Makarios' edicts were regarded as an attempt to impose controls on the growing security forces, the Greek Cypriot "warlords" and the independent armies that had often attacked Turkish Cypriots without authority from the central government. (The UN Security Council Feb. 28 received a report charging that more than 800 Turkish Cypriots had been killed or wounded since the fighting started in Cyprus Dec. 21, 1963. Rauf Denktash, president of Cyprus' Turkish communal chamber, told the Council that of 700 Turkish Cypriots who had been evacuated from the fighting zones, only 534 had been released. Denktash charged that the others had been shot and buried in mass graves.)

The first outbreak of fighting in March occurred on the northern coast in the Kyrenia area. A Turkish Cypriot was killed Mar. 5 in fighting at Kazaphani, east of Kyrenia. Other clashes raged that day in the Kyrenia-area towns of Ballapais, Karmi and Temblos. 5 Turkish Cypriots were injured Mar. 5 when a bomb exploded in the Turkish communal legislative chamber in Nicosia.

Violence spread to the southeast coast Mar. 7 with fighting in Paphos and in the nearby district village of Ktima. A cease-fire was arranged in Ktima Mar. 8 by Maj. Gen. Richard Carver, British UN truce commander, and Lt. Gen. Prem Singh Gyani of India, military commander of the proposed UN peace force for Cyprus. (Both men had been appointed to their posts under the Mar. 4 UN Security Council resolution that had set up the UN peace-keeping machinery.) British authorities reported that 6 Greek Cypriots and a Turkish Cypriot had been killed in the Paphos fighting. The Turks released 228 Greek hostages seized during the Paphos clashes but still held 55. (49 of 207 Turkish hostages had been released by Greeks in Nicosia Mar. 7 after Cyprus Pres. Makarios Mar. 6 had ordered that all hostages be turned over to the International Red Cross in Nicosia. Makarios had urged "a reciprocal response and gesture" by the Turkish Cypriots. In addition to the Paphos prisoners, 8 Greek Cypriots were said to be hostages, and 30 others were missing.)

Fighting resumed in the Paphos area Mar. 8 as Greeks surrounded the village of Mallia. Greeks Mar. 8 also overran Lapithou and seized more than 20 hostages. Greek Cypriot forces launched another attack in Paphos Mar. 9 and cut off the town by setting up roadblocks. The Greeks halted their offensive later in the evening to arrange for the evacuation of women and children from the fighting zone. The town's Turkish leader said 14 Turks were killed and 33 missing and presumed to be hostages of the Greeks. The Greek police chief said 3 Greek Cypriots were killed in the fighting. Vice Pres. Fazil Kutchuk urged the Turkish force in Paphos Mar. 9 to reject Greek conditions for ending the fighting. A Greek Cypriot said the demands called for the Turks to abandon and destroy their fortifications and "accept the authority of the legal forces to patrol the whole town, including the Turkish quarter, thus insuring the security of the whole population."

Turkish Cypriot fighters surrendered to a Greek force in Kazaphani Mar. 10, but British security troops moved into the village to protect the Turks. The Greeks demanded that the British withdraw or face the consequences. The Greeks later modified their demands and said the British troops could remain but not patrol the village. British troops also rushed into Mallia Mar. 10 after 2 Turkish Cypriots had been killed and others had surrendered that day to an overwhelming Greek force. As in Kazaphani, the Greeks warned the British to leave lest "an unpleasant situation arise." Because of the British intervention in Kazaphani and Mallia, Makarios Mar. 10 accused British forces of "protecting the Turkish rebels."

The Greek Cypriots informed British authorities Mar. 10 that they would no longer recognize the Dec. 1963 agreement that had established a truce line dividing the Greek and Turkish sectors of Nicosia. The truce boundary, known as the "green-line," had been agreed to by Britain, Greece, Turkey and the Greek and Turkish Cypriots to end the fighting in the city. The agreement empowered British security units patrolling the line to fire on intruders.

UN Secy. Gen. U Thant had warned Cyprus, Greece and Turkey Mar. 9 that continuance of the clashes "can only lead to even more tragic, widespread and deplorable consequences." Thant said his appeal was a renewal of his Feb. 15 plea to the 3 governments to use restraint; he said their responses then had been "positive." In reply to Thant's appeal, Makarios said Mar. 10 that "every effort is being made ... to avoid any act that might worsen the situation." Makarios, however, accused "Turkish extremists" of "deliberately creating incidents by armed action, endangering public safety and causing friction."

Vice Pres. Kutchuk Mar. 10 urged prompt UN intervention to save the Turkish Cypriots "from complete annihilation." In cablegrams sent to Thant and the foreign ministers of Greece, Turkey and Britain, Cyprus' guarantor powers, Kutchuk said: "If an effective UN force cannot be dispatched forthwith, we ... call upon the guarantor powers to fulfill their treaty obligations and rescue the Turks from the threat of genocide."

A 10-day lull in the communal fighting was broken Mar. 19 as Greek Cypriots, armed with mortars and bazookas, attacked the poorly-armed northern coastal Turkish Cypriot village of Ghaziveran. 3 Turks and a Greek were killed. British security authorities estimated that about 500 Greek Cypriots had surrounded the village Mar. 18 in preparation for the attack. According to the Greeks, the fighting started after the Turks rejected their demands for the removal of roadblocks. The Turks claimed the Greeks had insisted that they surrender their weapons. 2 cease-fires were agreed to and broken Mar. 19. The first truce was arranged by a small British security force that later left Ghaziveran. The fighting then resumed, and a 2d cease-fire was negotiated by Glafkos Clerides, Greek Cypriot president of the House of Representatives. British troops later reentered the village to reinforce the truce.

Sporadic clashes were reported Mar. 20 in Kalokhorio, southwest of Ghaziveran, and at Temblos, a Turkish village that continued to resist a Greek siege. Deserted Turkish Cypriot homes were set afire in Kato Koutrapha and in Ayios Epiphanious Mar. 20.

Turkey had called Mar. 19 for a halt in the new outbreak of fighting. The appeal was made in messages sent to UN Secy. Gen. U Thant, Pres. Makarios and Lt. Gen. Prem Singh Gyani, commander of the UN peace-keeping force. Turkish Premier Ismet Inonu asserted Mar. 20 that "large-scale preparations are being made and large-scale fighting is imminent in those areas [in Cyprus] where none has occurred previously." Inonu warned that if heavy fighting resumed and the Turkish Cypriot minority faced annihilation, "such a thing would leave us no choice but to intervene." Inonu repeated Turkish demands for a federal state in Cyprus with a shifting of the Greek and Turkish populations.

UN Troops Arrive, Turkey Drops Invasion Plan

The first contingent of the UN peace-keeping force flew to Cyprus Mar. 14, 1964. The dispatch of the UN soldiers — 27 Canadians — resulted in Turkey's withdrawal of a Mar. 13 threat to invade Cyprus to protect the minority Turkish Cypriot community.

The Canadian soldiers were the advance party for 1,150 approved by the Ottawa government. They were to form the nucleus of a 7,000-man force made up of soldiers from Finland, Sweden and Ireland and the 3,500-member British security force already in Cyprus. The Canadians awaited instructions from UN headquarters in New York before taking an active role in keeping the peace since the exact function of the force had not yet been determined.

UN Secy. Gen. U Thant, who had been working to get troops for the force since Mar. 4, had announced Mar. 13 that he had received "firm and official assurances" from Canada, Sweden and Ireland that they would furnish men and that the Canadians were on their way to Cyprus. (Finland's promise was received Mar. 14.) Thant's announcement was made before a UN Security Council emergency session that had been requested that day by Cyprus with a charge of a "clear threat of imminent invasion" of Cyprus by "Turkish forces." The Council unanimously approved a resolution urging all sides in the dispute to refrain from aggravating the situation and calling on Thant to continue to seek implementation of the Mar. 4 Council resolution that provided for the UN peace-keeping force. The Mar. 13 resolution was drawn up by Brazil, Bolivia, the Ivory Coast, Morocco and Norway.

The Turkish government said later Mar. 13 that it welcomed Thant's announcement that UN soldiers were on their way to Cyprus and that it would contribute $100,000 for the UN force.

The Turkish announcement was, in effect, a retraction of a threatening note it had sent to Pres. Makarios earlier Mar. 13. The note had charged that Greek Cypriot "aggression against the Turks on the island has taken such a turn that it obliges all humanity to rebel." Ankara demanded an end to "all kinds of individual or collective aggression, massacre, sacking, rebelling and rape and torture." It insisted on "the lifting of all sieges, the granting of free movement, the release of hostages and the return of bodies of the slain [Turkish Cypriots]." The note warned that unless its demands were met, Turkey would "use its unilateral [military] intervention granted by the agreement of Aug. 1960" that had established Cyprus as an independent state.

(The Turkish note also was handed to the U.S., British and Greek ambassadors, and a copy was sent to Thant.) To back up its threats of an invasion, Turkey had undertaken these military measures: Its air force assumed control of the civilian airfield at the Mediterranean port of Iskenderun; jet planes made regular flights along the sea corridor between Turkey and Cyprus; troops sealed off all roads leading to Iskenderun; an area just south of the port was used as a staging area; naval units were massed off the Turkish coast.

Makarios, who had been in Athens to attend King Paul's funeral, cut short his visit and returned to Nicosia Mar. 13 and ordered the rejection of the Turkish note. The Cyprus government's reply to Ankara called the note "a further untenable interference in the internal affairs of Cyprus." Asserting that Cyprus had not encouraged attacks on Turkish Cypriots, the Nicosia reply said that "no assaults or other acts such as those alleged in the [Turkish] note are being committed, no sieges exist, no hostages kept."

Turkish Amb.-to-Cyprus Mazhar Ozkol refused to accept the Cyprus government's reply on the ground that Turkey "was not expecting an answer but simply wanted to know whether the Turkish government demands would be immediately fulfilled."

Returning to Nicosia, Makarios said he was puzzled by the Turkish charges. He asserted that "despite Turkish Cypriot provocations which are systematically fomented from abroad, the security forces have displayed much self-restraint.' Makarios said he was further baffled by Ankara's accusations because the communal fighting in Cyprus had subsided and the UN was making progress in recruiting the peace force. Makarios charged that the Turkish Cypriots were "trying to create a situation that would give the Turkish government a pretext for intervention."

Greece, which had alerted its forces Mar. 13 to counteract the Turkish threat, announced Mar. 14 that despite Ankara's decision to refrain from military action "the emergency will continue until the international force arrives in Cyprus and is able to guarantee peace."

British Foreign Secy. R. A. Butler had appealed Mar. 13 to Turkish Amb. Zeiki Kunerlap to urge his government not to intervene in Cyprus because the UN apparently was near success in recruiting a peace force.

Tuomioja Appointed UN Mediator

Secy. Gen. U Thant designated Finnish Amb.-to-Sweden Sakari Severi Tuomioja, 52, as UN mediator in Cyprus. Thant announced the appointment officially Mar. 25, 1964 and said it had been approved by Cyprus, Greece, Turkey and Britain. Unanimous approval by the 4 nations was required under the Mar. 4 UN Security Council resolution that had established the UN force for Cyprus. Tuomioja, a former Finnish premier, was given the task of going to Cyprus to try to work out a permanent solution of the dispute between the island's Greek and Turkish communities.

UN Force Starts Operations

The UN Force in Cyprus (UNFICYP) formally started operations Mar. 27, 1964 following ceremonies in Nicosia in which (a) Lt. Gen. Prem Syngh Gyani officially assumed command of the UN units, (b) the British flag was hauled down and replaced with the UN flag.

UNFICYP thus relieved the British security troops (on the island since Dec. 1963) of sole responsibility for the task of preventing further fighting between Greek and Turkish Cypriots. 3,500 troops of the British force joined 1,000 Canadians, who, thus far, were the only UN soldiers on the island. 30 Swedish troops arrived by U.S. Air Force transport in Cyprus Apr. 4 as the first members of a Swedish battalion assigned to the UN force. Some of the remaining British troops were to go back to Malta, the others were to return to their bases in Cyprus. (Canadian troops Mar. 27 relieved British soldiers in their positions in the Nicosia suburb of Trakhonas. Other Canadians Mar. 28 assumed control of the Kyrenia area on the northern coast.)

Cypriot Foreign Min. Kyprianou was reported Mar. 31 to have informed UN Secy. Gen. U Thant that his government would comply with a "status-of-force agreement" covering UNFICYP operations pending Cyprus' formal ratification of the pact. The agreement included authorization for the use of UN flags and identification markings and freedom of UN troop movement and distribution of supplies. The UN announced Mar. 31 that Cyprus had contributed $280,000 (in cash and supplies) for UNFICYP's upkeep. Total pledges for UNFICYP received thus far: $5,189,000. (Switzerland had announced a $75,000 contribution Mar. 26.)

U Thant had said Apr. 1 that he had instructed UNFICYP troops not to shoot except in self-defense and to interpose themselves to stop any fighting between Greek and Turkish Cypriots. Specific operational instructions for the UN force were outlined Apr. 13 in a memo issued by Thant: UNFICYP units were to go to any scene of a potential clash, and the local commander was to try to get both sides to withdraw. "If all attempts at peaceful settlement fail," UNFICYP troops may "be deployed in such threatened areas" "in the interests of law and order." If, in the course of ensuing fighting, the safety of the UN troops were threatened, the UN soldiers "will defend themselves and their positions by resisting and driving off the attackers with a minimum of force." The UN troops were to warn beforehand of their intention to shoot. They were to use automatic weapons only "in extreme emergency" and they were to fire only as long as was required to achieve the "immediate aim." Where fighting was actually in progress, the local UNFICYP commander would attempt "to enforce a cease-fire by interposing" his soldiers between the engaging Cypriot forces but only if both sides agreed to the move or if there were no doubt as to its effectiveness.

A UN spokesman said Apr. 13 that Thant had asked the 5 UNFICYP countries (Britain, Canada, Ireland, Finland and Sweden) to augment the force by providing civilian policemen. The spokesman said Sweden had approved the proposal in principle and Britain had refused. The Swedish UN mission in New York had announced Apr. 10 that Stockholm had agreed to increase its UNFICYP troop contribution from 700 men to 1,000 in response to an Apr. 8 appeal by Thant. Thant asked Denmark Apr. 14 to provide a 600-man contingent for UNFICYP. The request was part of Thant's effort to reduce the number of British troops in the UN force. Reporting to the Security Council May 4 on the formation and operation of UNFICYP, Thant listed the force's strength as 6,341 military personnel and 28 civilian police, the latter sent by Austria. Thant said that an additional 1,000 troops were due from Denmark and 70 from Sweden. The additions, he said, would raise the force's strength to its planned level of 7,000 men by mid-May. The British contingent, the force's largest, was to be reduced to keep the total within 7,000. The following contingents were listed as serving with the force by Apr. 30: Austria — 10, Britain — 2,719, Canada — 1,087, Finland — 1,000, Ireland — 636, Sweden — 889.

Pres. Makarios and Gen. Gyani had reached agreement Apr. 4 on a plan for freedom of movement over Cyprus' 10 main trunk roads. The agreement included the border truce area, established in Dec. 1963, separating the Greek and Turkish communities in Nicosia. The plan called for the Turkish Cypriots to yield their positions to UNFICYP troops and Greek Cypriot police. The Turkish Cypriots Apr. 6 proposed another plan under which they would give up their positions only to UNFICYP troops. In a note to Gyani, Vice Pres. Kutchuk proposed that (a) UNFICYP troops patrol the main roads to guarantee freedom of movement, (b) UNFICYP troops hold fortified posts where the roads enter towns, (c) Turkish policemen continue to control Turkish areas. (Makarios had said Mar. 31 that he was agreeable to having all Greek Cypriots except the regular police disarmed under UNFICYP supervision if the Turkish Cypriots also disarmed. Gen. Gyani had asked Kutchuk Mar. 31 to arrange the dismantling of an airstrip that Turkish Cypriots were building near Krini. Kutchuk said he would do so only if UNFICYP could control Greek arms shipments.)

UN-led British soldiers had come under fire in 2 separate actions Mar. 30: (1) A 12-man patrol was trapped for nearly 3 hours by gunfire in the Greek village of Halevga, 12 miles northeast of Nicosia; the British made their way out of the area after

firing about 100 rounds of ammunition; Greek Cypriot authorities later acknowledged the shooting and said the British soldiers
had been mistaken for Turkish terrorists. (2) Greek Cypriots
fired twice on a British troop position in the Kamiakli Kutchuk
(Omorphita) district in northern Nicosia.

Joint patrols of UNFICYP's British troops and Greek
Cypriot police began operating in Nicosia and the surrounding
countryside Apr. 2 to guarantee the cease-fire in the area. But in
northwest Cyprus, in the village of Ayia Marinna, UN officials
said Greek Cypriots pinned down British paratroopers of
UNFICYP with gunfire during a battle Apr. 3 in which a Greek
and a Turkish Cypriot were reported killed and 2 Turks
wounded. UN officials blamed the firing on Greek Cypriot police
and "irregulars."

Turks in the west Cyprus village of Kokkina and Greeks in
the nearby hamlet of Pakhyammos agreed to a cease-fire Apr. 6
under UNFICYP supervision; the fighting, which had been in
progress for 3 days in the area, stopped later Apr. 6. But outside
Nicosia, Greek Cypriots took 4 Turkish Cypriot prisoners to a
field Apr. 6 and shot them. 2 were reported killed, one wounded
and one missing. Turkish Cypriot officials said the shootings
apparently were in reprisal for the killing of a Greek Cypriot
auxiliary policeman in Nicosia Apr. 5.

Makarios Abrogates 1960 Defense Pact

Pres. Makarios announced Apr. 4, 1964 that Cyprus had
terminated the 3-power Cypriot-Turkish-Greek common-defense
treaty, known as the Treaty of Alliance. The treaty, signed July
6, 1960, had been one of the accords under which Britain granted
Cyprus independence. It permitted Turkey to base 650 troops
and Greece 950 in Cyprus. Makarios summoned Turkish Amb.
Mazhar Ozkol to the presidential palace in Nicosia Apr. 4 and
handed him a note informing Turkish Premier Ismet Inonu of
Cyprus' repudiation of the treaty. The note, explaining the Cypriot action, said that the treaty had been violated by Turkey
when its troops had left their barracks on the edge of Nicosia
Dec. 25, 1963 to defend a besieged Turkish Cypriot enclave north

of Nicosia. Makarios had demanded that Turkey return the troops to their barracks, but Inonu had refused to do so until the protection of the Turkish minority was guaranteed. Makarios pointed out that Turkish troops were stationed in Cyprus under the Treaty of Alliance not to protect the Turkish minority but solely for "common defense."

The Turkish government, after a cabinet meeting Apr. 5, rejected the treaty's termination as illegal. Inonu denounced Makarios' action as another attempt to abrogate the treaty unilaterally. Turkish Foreign Min. Feridun Cemal Erkin said the treaty had no provision for unilateral abrogation. (Cypriot Vice Pres. Fazil Kutchuk said in a message to Inonu Apr. 5 that the treaty could not be abrogated without his approval.)

Makarios had said Jan. 1 that he intended to abrogate the 3-power Treaty of Alliance and the 4-power Treaty of Guarantee, both included in the constitutional provisions signed July 6, 1960. But his Apr. 4 note referred only to the Treaty of Alliance. The Treaty of Guarantee, signed by Cyprus, Britain, Greece and Turkey, guaranteed the protection of the Turkish minority; and, under the treaty, Britain, Greece and Turkey pledged common action to prevent any merger or partition of Cyprus. Glafkos Clerides, president of the Cypriot parliament, had warned that Cyprus would ask the UN to abrogate both the Treaty of Guarantee and the Treaty of Alliance if Sakari S. Tuomioja, the UN mediator, failed to achieve a lasting settlement. Cypriot Foreign Min. Spyros A. Kyprianou informed UN Secy. Gen. U Thant Apr. 6 that Cyprus had decided to terminate the Treaty of Alliance.

(The Turkish Chamber of Deputies and Senate had held a joint session Mar. 16 and had unanimously approved Pres. Inonu's request for full power to implement Turkey's right under the 1960 Cyprus treaty of guarantee to intervene if he considered it necessary. The joint legislative session abrogated a 1930 treaty that provided privileged treatment for 10,000 Greek nationals who lived in Turkey. Greece feared the Turkish action was designed to force Greek concessions in Cyprus, and Athens asked Ankara for an explanation. A Turkish Foreign Ministry official Mar. 17 said the abrogation of the 1930 treaty had "nothing whatever to do with the Cyprus crisis" and had been contemplated for a long time by the Turkish government.)

The Cypriot government warned Apr. 7 that it would take steps to drive Turkish troops off the island. Makarios said that as an initial measure the government would "stop granting to the Turkish military force the facilities provided for under the Treaty of Alliance." He said he would appeal to the UN Security Council if Turkish troops were not withdrawn "eventually." (It was reported Apr. 7 that the Turkish ambassador in Athens had informed Greek Foreign Min. Stavros Costopoulos that Turkey would invade Cyprus, if necessary, to protect its garrison there.) Makarios said he had ordered a cut-off of water, electricity and fuel for the Turkish garrison. He said the facilities would not be restored until Turkish troops relinquished their control of the key Nicosia-Kyrenia road and returned to their barracks. He threatened to use force to free the road from Turkish control.

Bunche Confers in Nicosia

UN Undersecy. for Political Affairs Ralph Bunche Apr. 9, 1964 began a series of talks in Nicosia with Greek and Turkish Cypriot leaders in an effort to find a solution to the dispute between the 2 ethnic communities. Bunche held separate discussions with Pres. Makarios and with Vice Pres. Kutchuk and 3 other Turkish Cypriot government ministers. After the Bunche-Makarios meeting, a government communique merely said that the 2 men had discussed the Cyprus situation "and the task of the UN force on the island." Although there was no official comment on Bunche's meeting with Kutchuk, the Turkish Cypriot officials were said to have complained to Bunche about the "passive attitude" of the UN peace-keeping force (UNFICYP). Bunche also conferred with Lt. Gen. Prem Singh Gyani, UNFICYP commander, Sakari S. Tuomioja, UN political mediator, and other UN officials.

Bunche met again with Makarios Apr. 10 and later toured the Nicosia truce line dividing the city's Greek and Turkish communities.

A Turkish Cypriot official news bulletin Apr. 10 called on Bunche to "make every effort to remedy the tragic situation" of the Turkish Cypriots. The bulletin reiterated Turkish Cypriot charges of UNFICYP's "passive attitude," which, it claimed, had "only served to encourage" Greek Cypriot "terrorists in police uniform to continue their brutal crimes on an ever larger scale" against the Turks.

Bunche, accompanied Apr. 11 by Gyani, visited Paphos, scene of bitter fighting in March. Bunche and his party were greeted in the city's Turkish quarter by about 300 demonstrators, many of whom carried placards assailing Gyani and UNFICYP.

Bunche ended his mission Apr. 12. Before leaving Cyprus, he called the Greek-Turkish Cypriot clashes "an incoherent war." Bunche said UNFICYP's principal aim was to "get a full hold on the situation" and stop the fighting.

Greece Seeks Independent Cyprus

A campaign to win complete independence for Cyprus through self-determination procedure was announced Apr. 13, 1964 by Greek Premier George Papandreou in a 10-point policy statement. He issued the pronouncement after conferring with Pres. Makarios in Athens Apr. 11-13. Makarios, present when Papandreou outlined his policy, said "I endorse everything the Greek premier says." Papandreou said in his policy statement:

(1) Greece supported the Greek Cypriots' "just struggle."

(2) "Greece's policy is peace, but in case of attack we shall defend ourselves."

(3) The 1960 treaty that established Cyprus as an independent state was inapplicable as proven by the fact that a UN force was on the island and a UN mediator had been appointed to seek a political solution.

(4) Makarios' termination of the Cypriot-Turkish-Greek common defense treaty merely confirmed the reality of the situation.

(5) Greece supported the UN force in Cyprus and "agreed to bring the Greek army contingent [on Cyprus] under the order of its commander."

(6) "We shall support" the UN mediator in Cyprus.

(7) The "only possible solution to the Cyprus problem" was "the application . . . of the principles of international justice and a true democracy." A government in which "the small [Turkish] minority of 18% imposes its will on the majority of 80% is . . . not a democracy. It is a conquest." The rights of the Turkish minority on Cyprus could be safeguarded with the aid of the UN.

(8) The only solution to the problem was complete independence for Cyprus to permit it to determine its own future.

(9) The Cyprus situation would be placed before the UN General Assembly if the UN mediator failed to find a solution.

(10) Greece's "keen desire is to preserve excellent relations with . . . Turkey. We regret deeply anti-Greek measures adopted by the Turkish government."

Turkey Accuses Greek Cypriots

Turkey charged in a note to UN Secy. Gen. U Thant Apr. 15, 1964 (made public Apr. 20) that Greek Cypriot government acts against the Turkish minority on Cyprus posed "a continuing danger to international peace and security." The note, filed by Turkish delegate to UN Orhan Eralp, warned that Ankara would submit the matter to the UN Security Council "if the above-mentioned danger to peace shows no sign of being abated."

In his note Eralp said: Greek Cypriots had attacked the Turkish minority on 5 occasions since the UN force was authorized Mar. 4 to help restore order; there had been other incidents involving "murder, abduction, looting and wanton and systematic destruction of private property"; "Greek Cypriot authorities" were "harassing and rendering helpless and hopeless the Turkish community on the island" in a policy of "piecemeal annihilation"; Greek Cypriot armed "irregular bands," posing falsely as "security forces," were "a grave danger to peace"; the forcible exclusion from the Cypriot government of Vice Pres. Kutchuk and of 3 Turkish Cypriot cabinet members made the current Nicosia regime unlawful; Pres. Makarios' statements on an Apr. 12-14 trip he had made to Athens proved that he had "now finally discarded the pretense of 'independence for Cyprus,' 'self-determination' and all the other stepping stones to his ultimate objective of union with Greece."

Makarios had conferred near Athens Apr. 12 and 14 with Gen. George Grivas, who had led Greek Cypriot resistance during Britain's occupation of the island. The discussions dealt with the possible return of Grivas to Cyprus to accept a Cyprus government offer to head the Greek Cypriot security forces. The Greek government was said to have pressured Grivas to reject the offer. Commenting on his talks with the general, Makarios said Apr. 15 that Grivas "does not think it expedient to go to Cyprus at present, probably because the situation is not grave." (Discussing other aspects of the Cyprus dispute, Makarios said U.S. policy would "become satisfactory" if Washington followed "democratic principles in this case . . . as in other cases." Makarios accused Turkey of having "encouraged and directed" Turkish Cypriot "provocations," which he claimed, were aimed at partition.)

The Turkish statement followed a series of violent clashes between Greek and Turkish Cypriots earlier in April:

● Greek Cypriot security forces had shot and killed a Turkish Cypriot and wounded his daughter Apr. 10 in the garden of their home on the truce line in a Nicosia suburb. A Turkish Cypriot policeman was killed by Greek gunfire near the truce line Apr. 11.

● Greek and Turkish Cypriots exchanged gunfire Apr. 11-13 in the Kyrenia mountain range despite UNFICYP truce team efforts to end the fighting. The shooting centered around the Kyrenia Pass area overlooking the strategic 12-mile Nicosia-Kyrenia road. The pass and the road were both controlled by Turkish Cypriots and Turkish army troops. A UNFICYP commander reported that Greek Cypriots had massed a force of about 500 men in the mountains in preparation for a drive to oust the Turks. The Turkish Cypriots Apr. 13 seized an unoccupied Kyrenia peak that overlooked the 2 Greek village strongholds of Pano and Kato Dhikomo. The purpose of the maneuver was to consolidate the Turkish hold on the Kyrenia Pass and the Nicosia-Kyrenia road. The Turkish force refused to quit the strategic height despite a Greek Cypriot threat to use mortars to recapture the hill and a UNFICYP truce team plea to abandon the position.

● Gunfire in Nicosia Apr. 14 resulted in the death of 2 Greek Cypriots and the wounding of 2 Greek Cypriots and a Turkish Cypriot. A Turkish army camp was fired on in the Nicosia suburb of Orta Keuy.

UN officials succeeded Apr. 19 in persuading Greek and Turkish Cypriot leaders to accept the neutralization of a disputed 1/2-square-mile area near the Nicosia truce line between the 2 communities. The zone, located immediately to the west of the old walled city of Nicosia, included a hotel, the UN force's headquarters, the British High Commission's building and the residence of UN mediator Tuomioja. It had been the scene of attempts by Greek and Turkish Cypriots to establish strongpoints; one of these, a Greek Cypriot post in front of the hotel, had been abandoned on Makarios' orders Apr. 18 when he visited the hotel. The agreement had called for both sides to withdraw most of their forces from the area and permit the UN to occupy their positions. UN spokesmen announced Apr. 21 that neutralization of the area had been postponed due to a deadlock on the procedure of withdrawal. It was understood, however, that Turkish Cypriot leaders had objected to measures that would have resulted in Greek Cypriot occupation of their (the Turks') parts of the area. Talks were resumed on the matter Apr. 22, but the agreement was not carried out.

A presidential statement issued by Makarios in Nicosia Apr. 22 offered Turkish Cypriots a general amnesty for crimes allegedly committed during the fighting if they joined Greek Cypriots in ending the island's strife. Makarios said that Greek Cypriots were prepared to dismantle all their military posts under UN supervision if Turkish Cypriots agreed to do the same. He said the Cyprus government then would assist Turkish Cypriots in returning to their homes and would guarantee them "protection for their lives and property." The amnesty was intended to assure the Turkish Cypriots against retaliatory prosecution for excesses committed during the fighting. Makarios warned that "if the Turkish Cypriot leadership does not show the necessary understanding," "no doubt" would remain that it had instigated the Cyprus violence on the orders of the Turkish government to create justification for Cyprus' partition and Turkish military intervention on the island. In that event he said, "we shall have to face the situation by all means."

Turkish Cypriot leaders rejected Makarios' declaration the same day. Cyprus Defense Min. Osman Orek, speaking for Vice Pres. Kutchuk and other Turkish Cypriot leaders at a Nicosia news conference Apr. 22, denounced the amnesty offer as "propaganda" and an attempt to get Turkish Cypriots "to admit that

we are all guilty." Orek declared that the Turkish Cypriot
community was "fighting to defend its life and property
against ... brutal attacks" and that it could not dismantle its
defensive positions so long as "40,000 unlawful armed" Greek
Cypriots were at the government's orders for attacks on the Turkish Cypriot community.

Battle for Kyrenia Castle

The Turkish Cypriot rejection of Makarios' amnesty offer
was followed by a major Greek Cypriot assault Apr. 25-28
against St. Hilarion Castle, the last major Turkish Cypriot
stronghold in northeastern Cyprus. Makarios ordered a cease-fire
Apr. 29 following a protest from Gen. Gyani, commander of the
UN Force. The castle, a 10th century crusaders' fortress,
dominated the principal pass through the Kyrenia mountain
range and the strategic Kyrenia-Nicosia highway.

The Greek Cypriot force, variously estimated at 300 to 1,500
men, had attacked Turkish Cypriot posts on high ground west of
the castle Apr. 25. Using automatic arms and mortars, the
attackers overran the defenders' posts and advanced to within
1/2 mile of the castle (2 miles by road) in the first day's fighting.
The attack threatened the emergency airstrip built by Turkish
Cypriots at the foot of the Kyrenia mountains and forced the
evacuation of 5 villages south of the mountains. The villagers
were taken to Guenyeli, the main base of the 650-man Turkish
army contingent on Cyprus.

A coordinated assault, reportedly commanded by Cyprus
Interior Min. Polykarpos Georghadjis, was directed against the
castle Apr. 27. The main body of Greek Cypriots was supported
by 2 other columns that attacked Turkish Cypriot outposts on
ridges east and north of the castle. The Greek Cypriots were
reported to have mortar-bombed at least one Turkish village
below the castle's heights. But the attackers failed to dislodge the
Turkish Cypriots from their positions around and in the castle
before the fighting ebbed Apr. 28. (Despite the violence of the
fighting, fatalities apparently were limited to 6 Turkish Cypriots
and 3 Greek Cypriots, all reported killed the first day of the
attack.)

The Cyprus government publicly acknowledged Apr. 29 that it commanded the Greek Cypriot forces surrounding the castle. A government communique issued in Nicosia said that the Greek Cypriots had been ordered to stop firing because "the object of the operation in the area has already been achieved." "Greek villages in the area have been rid of Turkish terrorism," it said "and the security forces, having stabilized their positions, are now controlling the area." Turkish Cypriot leaders ridiculed the communique. They said the Greek attack had been intended to take the castle and free the Nicosia-Kyrenia highway from Turkish control but had failed.

Gen. Gyani had said Apr. 28 that he had warned Makarios that the assault had "serious implications regarding the obligations of the [Cyprus] government and the role of the United Nations force." Gyani, who also had conferred with Georghadjis about his personal role in the attack, said that it apparently had been "pre-planned" in violation of Cypriot government pledges to prevent further outbreaks of violence. Gyani reported to UN Secy. Gen. U Thant on the Kyrenia attack Apr. 28. His report was not made public, but it was said to have urged a reassessment of the UN force's operating orders. Canadian units of the UN force had been in the Kyrenia area during the Greek Cypriot attack but had not intervened in force because their officers believed their troops risked unnecessary casualties if they interposed themselves between the 2 sides. The Canadians had attempted to place several armored cars between the attackers and defenders but apparently had withdrawn them when it became clear that neither side would cease fire.

The UN's failure to halt the attack immediately had been interpreted by Turkish Cypriots as favoritism by Gyani to the Greek Cypriots. Gyani had been turned back by a mob when he sought to enter the Turkish quarters of Nicosia Apr. 26 to confer with Vice Pres. Kutchuk. He returned later the same day with a Turkish Cypriot police escort, but as he left the meeting with Kutchuk a Turkish Cypriot mob surrounded his car, stoned it and shouted death threats at him. Many Turkish Cypriots were reported to believe that Gyani's alleged partiality toward the Greek Cypriots was connected with India's known opposition to Turkish proposals for Cyprus' partition.

(The *N.Y. Times* reported May 6 that the St. Hilarion fighting had brought widespread foreign condemnation of the Cyprus government for its responsibility for the attack. Greek Premier Papandreou was said to have telephoned Makarios to ask him to order the assaulting forces to cease fire.)

The Kyrenia fighting had been preceded by an outbreak of clashes Apr. 23 in the mixed village of Ayios Theodoros in southern Cyprus. The UN-imposed truce there was broken by heavy firing that went on intermittently for a week. 3 platoons of British troops under UN command were sent to the village Apr. 23 to reinforce Britons already on the scene, but they failed to halt the renewed fighting. 2 Turkish Cypriots were killed and several Greek Cypriots severely wounded in the village by Apr. 28. Much of the shooting was directed at and from a village school where Turkish Cypriot women and children had been gathered and a Turkish gun post had been established. The British troops established a UN post in the school Apr. 25 and persuaded the armed Turkish Cypriots to leave the building the next day to assure the safety of the women and children

Thant's Peace Plan

In the wake of the accelerated fighting on the island, UN Secy. Gen. U Thant proposed Apr. 29, 1964 a peace plan that called for the appointment of a "top-level" political officer appointed by the UN to negotiate an interim accord based on the Secretary General's proposals. Major points of Thant's plan: (a) The removal of all fortified positions built by Greek and Turkish Cypriots, beginning in the Nicosia area. (b) The disarming of all civilians and the limitation of weapons to members of the Cypriot police and gendarmerie. (c) The restoration of freedom of movement on all roads and within Cyprus' towns and cities. (d) A general amnesty and the restoration of judicial law and order. (e) Reintegration of Turkish Cypriots into the Cyprus government and its police and other services. (f) The return of refugees to their homes, beginning in the Nicosia area, under UN force protection. (g) The possible formation of joint Greek-Turkish-UN patrols to restore order and confidence.

In submitting his plan to the UN Security Council, Thant warned that the Greek and Turkish Cypriot community leaders must act "urgently" and responsibly "to bring completely to an end the fighting...if that island country is to avoid utter disaster." Thant urged Pres. Makarios and Vice Pres. Kutchuk to call publicly for compliance with the Mar. 4 Security Council resolution asking for an end to the violence. He indicated that a solution based on armed action by the UN Force in Cyprus was unacceptable: "It would be...a little insane," he said, "for that force to set about killing Cypriots, whether Greek or Turkish, to prevent them from killing each other." Thant's report criticized the Cyprus government's involvement in the attack on St. Hilarion Castle. The report called the assault "especially serious since it clearly was a planned and organized military effort."

Thant drew up his plan after receiving a report Apr. 28 from UN mediator Sakari S. Tuomioja on his talks the previous week with Greek, Turkish and Cypriot leaders. Tuomioja had conferred in Athens Apr. 26-28 with King Constantine, Premier George Papandreou and Foreign Min. Stavros Costopoulos. He conceded to newsmen before leaving Athens that he had made little progress in his meetings with the Greek rulers or in his earlier meetings with Turkish leaders. Tuomioja had returned to Cyprus Apr. 19 after 3 days of talks with Premier Ismet Inonu and other Turkish officials in Ankara. Makarios had conferred with Tuomioja in Nicosia Apr. 20 and had warned the following day that Turkish proposals to partition the island were unacceptable to the Greek Cypriot majority. Interviewed by the Athens newspaper *To Vima*, Makarios said that Turkey had suggested that Cyprus be turned into a federated republic in which the Turkish Cypriot state would be given 38% of the island's territory and the Greek Cypriot state would occupy the remainder. Makarios added: "This is quite unacceptable. It cannot even be discussed."

Implementing a major plank of his peace plan, Thant May 11 appointed Galo Plaza Lasso, ex-president of Ecuador, as his special representative for direct negotiations with the Greek and Turkish Cypriots. Plaza was directed to open talks with the leaders of the 2 warring Cypriot communities to bring an end to hostilities and a return to normal conditions. Plaza's appointment was intended to free Lt. Gen. Prem Singh Gyani, UN Force commander, for military matters. UN officials said Plaza's functions would not conflict with those of Tuomioja, who was charged with seeking a long-term political solution. Plaza arrived in Cyprus May 14 to take up his duties. He returned to New York May 19 to report to U Thant on the results of his first contacts with the leaders of Cyprus' Greek and Turkish communities.

(The Ministerial Council of the Central Treaty Organization [CENTO], meeting in Washington Apr. 28-29, had called for an immediate end to the communal strife in Cyprus. The council, in a communique issued Apr. 29, expressed "deep concern" and warned that continued unrest on the island would have "grave implications for peace and security in the whole area." The meeting, attended by the foreign ministers of the 4 CENTO powers [Britain, Turkey, Iran and Pakistan] and by U.S. State Secy. Dean Rusk, was said to have been disrupted by the smaller states' warnings that they considered themselves threatened by non-Communist neighbors as much as by the Soviet bloc. Turkish Foreign Min. Feridun C. Erkin was reported to have warned at the Apr. 28 session that Cyprus could become the "Cuba of the Mediterranean" unless the strife was settled. Pres. Johnson conferred privately with each of the visiting foreign ministers Apr. 29. Erkin told reporters after his meeting with Mr. Johnson that Turkey expected the UN Force to "intervene more actively" to restore order on the island.)

Fighting Shatters Truce

An informal truce interrupted the Cyprus fighting May 1, 1964, but the truce was broken May 11 with the slaying of 2 Greek army officers in Famagusta. The truce had been proposed by Greek Cypriot leaders in connection with the opening May 1 of the 4-day Greek Orthodox Easter holiday. The cease-fire was observed by both sides except for some minor incidents. It was prolonged after the UN Force had taken advantage of the lull to establish new positions in certain key areas, most importantly between the Greek Cypriot and Turkish Cypriot forces deployed in the area of St. Hilarion Castle, overlooking the Kyrenia Pass and the Nicosia-Kyrenia highway. (3 Turkish Cypriots had been killed near St. Hilarion Apr. 30 in a new outbreak of shooting, the last in the area before the holiday.)

2 key peace-keeping actions by the UN Force were believed to have contributed to the effectiveness of the holiday truce:

●In the first, Swedish UN troops patrolling near the village of Timi, on Cyprus' south coast, disarmed a group of Greek Cypriot irregulars that had opened fire on the UN patrol. The Greek Cypriots were said to have fired more than 2,000 shots at the Swedes from positions in the Timi village, but they surrendered after 4 armored cars entered the village. The Swedes disarmed 40 irregulars and turned their weapons over to Cypriot police in nearby Paphos. This was the first time UN troops had disarmed a band of Cypriots. No casualties were reported.

●In the 2d action, UN units, supported by armored cars, established 12 permanent guardposts in the St. Hilarion area. The posts were situated at the entrance to the castle and in strategic positions near both Greek and Turkish Cypriot emplacements and in Turkish villages near the scene of the fighting.

Minor skirmishes were reported between Greek Cypriots and Turkish Cypriots May 6 in Trakhonas, a Nicosia suburb, and in Famagusta, on the east coast, but both clashes were halted by UN patrols. Heavy fighting was reported to have broken out May 8 near the village of Louroujina, southeast of Nicosia, but British UN units intervened and forced the opposing forces to withdraw from range of each other.

The 2 Greek army officers slain May 11 in Famagusta were shot down by unknown assailants, presumably Turkish Cypriots, as they drove through the city's Turkish quarter. Their Greek Cypriot driver, Costas Pantelides, a policeman and son of the Nicosia police chief, was also killed. Sporadic shooting broke out in the Famagusta area after the killings, and at least 9 Turkish Cypriots were reported to have been abducted by armed Greek Cypriots. Irish UN units were sent to the city, however, and succeeded in restoring order by May 12. (The Greek government denounced the slayings, but the Greek Defense Ministry announced May 12 that the Greek army garrison on Cyprus had been ordered to avoid any retaliatory action.)

During the truce, Cyprus remained calm except for sporadic gunfire reported May 8 in the Turkish Cypriot village of Louroujina, 12 miles southeast of Nicosia, and May 9 in Nicosia and the Kyrenia mountain area between Nicosia and Kyrenia.

A soldier of the Finnish contingent serving with the UN Force was killed by gunfire May 20 near the Turkish Cypriot village of Kara Tepe, northwest of Nicosia on the Nicosia-Kyrenia highway. He was the first UN soldier to be killed in a combat situation in Cyprus.

The UN command was reported May 16 to have ordered its troops to shoot if necessary to protect Cypriot civilians. The new orders were said to have been issued to help UN contingents deal with new violence expected with the beginning of the harvest season. The orders reportedly were communicated to Pres. Makarios and Vice Pres. Kutchuk May 16 by special UN emissary Galo Plaza Lasso. UN troops formerly had been limited to firing in self-defense. Lt. Gen. Prem Singh Gyani, commander of the UN force, had toured the Famagusta dock area May 15 with Makarios and had berated the Greek Cypriot district officer publicly for acts of violence reported against Turkish Cypriots in Famagusta. Gyani particularly protested the presence on the waterfront of a Greek Cypriot guard post with automatic weapons pointed at the Irish UN guard in the area. Makarios had expressed similar views of Greek Cypriot responsibility for the violence during a "pacification tour" of western Cyprus May 7. Speaking to members of both communities in the mixed village of Timi, Makarios had heard Turkish Cypriots' complaints of attacks by their neighbors and had conceded that "up to a point they are justified." (On a visit to Limassol the previous day, Makarios had inspected a secret Greek Cypriot arms factory and had said at a rally of cheering Greek Cypriots that his aim was "full independence" for Cyprus.)

The NATO Council in Paris had held a special session on the Cyprus problem on Turkish request May 2. Turkish Amb.-to-NATO Nuri Birgi protested the attacks on Turkish Cypriots and charged the Greek government with encouraging and supporting the Cyprus strife. Greek Amb.-to-NATO Christos Palamas responded with similar charges against Turkey. The Council took no action.

(The Greek air force announced May 5 that its planes had been ordered to intercept any Turkish aircraft violating Greek airspace; dispatches from Athens said the orders had been issued after Turkish planes flew near Greek destroyers on patrol. Athens sources reported May 12 that Greek armored forces had begun maneuvers in Thrace, adjacent to the Turkish border.)

The Cyprus government was reported May 18 to have taken steps toward the enactment of military conscription and the purchase of heavy military equipment abroad. The report, issued by the semi-official Cyprus news agency, was confirmed later May 18 by Pres. Glafkos Clerides of the Cyprus House of Representatives. According to the news agency, Cypriot envoys had opened negotiations for the purchase of the "necessary war equipment." It said that the government's decision to seek the arms had been dictated by the need to complete "preparations to face possible Turkish aggression" against Cyprus. The agency reported that the draft law would provide for conscription of 5 age groups to increase the strength of the Cypriot armed forces. The agency said the arms to be bought would include fighter and bomber planes, anti-aircraft and other heavy weapons and torpedo-boats. Clerides told newsmen that the report was true but that he could not provide information on where the arms were to be bought or on the specific terms of the conscription law. (Observers reported that the law was intended to regularize the status of the paramilitary force raised by the Greek Cypriot community since the Cyprus fighting began in Dec. 1963. The force currently was estimated at 15,000 to 30,000 men.)

Dispute over Hostages

The UN and the Cyprus government called May 16-17 for the immediate release of Turkish Cypriots taken hostage by Greek Cypriots, particularly since the slaying of 2 Greek army officers and a Greek Cypriot policeman in Famagusta. Makarios denounced the abductions of Turkish Cypriots. In a statement broadcast May 16, Makarios said that the Greek Cypriots responsible for the abductions had done "serious damage to their country" and its reputation. He warned that his government would take all measures necessary to put an end to abductions. Makarios' statement was made after 3 armed Greek Cypriots had kidnaped Hushref Suleiman, a Turkish reporter, in front of a Nicosia hotel. Suleiman was released after UN officials had interceded with Greek Cypriot officials on his behalf. A UN statement made public in Nicosia May 17 said that the UN expected Makarios' orders to lead to the swift release of all Turkish Cypriot hostages.

Despite the 2 statements, Makarios failed to secure the release of any of the hostages by May 19, when he conferred with Galo Plaza Lasso, U Thant's special emissary on the Cyprus problem. Makarios informed Plaza that only 17 Turkish hostages — of a reported total of 91 — were in the custody of the Cyprus government. He said that 7 of these had been cleared for release and that the 10 others would be freed as soon as it was known whether they were wanted on criminal charges connected with the fighting. He asserted that the government had no knowledge of the whereabouts of the 74 other reported hostages. Speaking with newsmen after his meeting with Makarios, Plaza said the Cyprus government appeared to be making a sincere effort to control the Greek Cypriot irregular forces. Plaza asserted that nearly all of the fighting that had occurred in Cyprus had been provoked by the irregulars of both communities.

Plaza conferred later May 19 with Vice Pres. Kutchuk to urge the release of 32 Greek Cypriots said to have been taken hostage. He reported that Kutchuk had denied that any hostages were known to be held currently by Turkish Cypriots.

U.S. Warns Turkey Against Invasion

The U.S. warned Turkey June 3 and 4, 1964 not to invade Cyprus. The warning was given in a message sent by Pres. Johnson to Turkish Premier Ismet Inonu and in a personal plea to Inonu by Gen. Lyman Lemnitzer, NATO commander. In his appeal to Inonu, Mr. Johnson urged the Turkish leader not to undertake any precipitous military action in the crisis and to come to Washington to discuss the matter with him. In a reply to Mr. Johnson June 9, Inonu said he was unable to visit the U.S. just then.

Mr. Johnson's plea was prompted by reports of Turkish plans to invade Cyprus June 6 (with a huge fleet reportedly massed at Iskenderun and at other ports along Turkey's southern coast) and the subsequent alert June 5 of the armed forces of Greece and Cyprus to counter any possible Turkish military intervention. Mr. Johnson's warning was said to have averted the invasion and to have eased the tension. Cyprus had mobilized 30,000 guardsmen and posted them along the northern coast facing Turkey and along the Greek-Turkish truce line in Nicosia. Cyprus canceled the alert June 6 as the threat of a Turkish invasion appeared to have abated.

Mr. Johnson's message was delivered to Inonu in Ankara by U.S. Amb.-to-Turkey Raymond A. Hare. In disclosing the note, a White House statement June 5 said the President's appeal was "only the latest step in a continuing pattern of consultation among allies." The U.S., the statement said, "has acted in full recognition that the role of peace-keeping and mediation on Cyprus belongs to the United Nations."

Gen. Lemnitzer June 4 flew from Paris to Ankara and conferred with Inonu, Gen. Cevdet Sunay, chief of staff, and other Turkish officials. Lemnitzer was said to have urged the Turks to consult their allies before taking any steps that might aggravate the Cyprus situation. Prior to meeting with Lemnitzer, Inonu had said in a broadcast June 4: "Our decision is final. We have to provide an unshakeable security for the future of the Cypriot Turks."

Inonu held an emergency cabinet meeting June 5 to consider the Johnson-Lemnitzer warnings and to review the Cyprus situation in general. Later, a statement by a Turkish government spokesman said Turkey had abandoned plans to land forces in Cyprus "for the time being." Inonu confirmed before the Turkish Senate June 18 that the U.S. appeals to Ankara had averted a Turkish plan to intervene militarily in Cyprus. Inonu said Turkish invasion plans had been readied since the middle of May because of Greece's announced support of Pres. Makarios' regime. Inonu said the planned Turkish invasion also had been aimed at averting what he called Cyprus' plans to massacre Turkish Cypriots. Inonu said that UN intervention in Cyprus had brought "no active result." (The Turkish National Assembly upheld Inonu's Cyprus policies June 19 by 200-194 vote [2 abstentions].)

Turkey's military moves had been prompted by a new political crisis between Cypriot Greeks and Turks in the Cyprus government. The Cypriot parliament (boycotted by Turkish Cypriot representatives) had passed controversial measures June 1 calling for: (1) conscription of 25,000 men into the National Guard; (2) unification of the police and gendarmerie into one force; (3) heavy purchases of arms from abroad. Employing his constitutional prerogative, Vice Pres. Fazil Kutchuk sent Pres. Makarios a letter in which he vetoed the bills. (Britain, Turkey and Greece had criticized all 3 measures.) Ignoring Kutchuk's veto, the Cyprus government June 4 began to induct Greek Cypriots aged 19-21 under the new conscription law.

Greek-Turkish tensions had been further heightened by Makarios' refusal June 3 of a request that day by Kutchuk to hold a cabinet meeting under UN auspices. Makarios said the demand had been made "exclusively for propaganda."

Sakari S. Tuomioja, UN political mediator in Cyprus, was recalled to New York June 3 to report to UN Secy. Gen. U Thant. On stopping over in Ankara June 4, Tuomioja said he had still been unable to find a solution to the Cyprus problem.

Lt. Gen. Prem Singh Gyani, commander of the UN Force in Cyprus (UNFICYP), had said in Nicosia May 28 that the force had accomplished some of its aims. But he said that "one of the major obstacles" faced by UNFICYP was "irresponsible and senseless conduct by armed men in both communities [Greek and Turkish] who don't appear to have any discipline or to be responsible to any established authority but have been acting on their own reckless initiative."

A Turkish government note (made public May 24) to Britain and Greece charged that the Cyprus government's "ultimate goal" was "the total annihilation" of the Turkish Cypriot community. Ankara said its charges were based on recent kidnappings of Turkish Cypriots and the Cyprus government's purchase of foreign arms and equipment.

Term of UN Force Extended

The UN Security Council June 20, 1964 unanimously approved the extension of the UN Force in Cyprus (UNFICYP) for another 3 months — from June 27 through Sept. 26. The June 20 resolution, drawn up by Brazil, Bolivia, the Ivory Coast, Morocco and Norway, reaffirmed Council resolutions of Mar. 4 and 13 that had established UNFICYP. At Cyprus' suggestion, Brazil inserted a paragraph calling on "all member states to comply with the above-mentioned resolutions." Cyprus Foreign Min. Spyros A. Kyprianou, who had attended the Council meetings, said at a news conference that the added paragraph was based on Cyprus' complaints that Turkey had ignored UN resolutions on Cyprus and had threatened to invade Cyprus.

Following the Council's extension of UNFICYP's term, UN Secy. Gen. U Thant appealed to its 9 contributory nations for continued financial aid to enable the force to maintain its operations. Thant also urged the countries to continue during the extra 3 months their participation in UNFICYP "at the same strength and on the same terms as at present." Thant had appointed Gen. Kodendera Subayya Thimayya, ex-chief of staff of the Indian army, to replace Lt. Gen. Prem Singh Gyani as UNFICYP commander. Gyani had asked to be replaced for personal reasons. Thant cabled Thimayya confirmation of his appointment after the Council vote. Thimayya assumed his new post July 8.

Cyprus Pres. Makarios June 20 called UNFICYP's extension "successful and satisfactory for Cyprus." Vice Pres. Fazil Kutchuk, Turkish Cypriot leader, was reported June 21 to be "neither pleased nor displeased" with UNFICYP's extension. At the same time Kutchuk was reported to have denounced a June 16 report to the Council in which Thant had requested the extension. In a note sent to Thant June 18, Kutchuk had charged that the report was "apparently written in either total ignorance or total disregard of the facts. The true state of affairs in Cyprus had not been reported to the Secretary General by United Nations officials [in Nicosia] in an unbiased and objective manner." Kutchuk cited Thant's report on the status of the Cyprus government, the importation and smuggling of arms and other topics as being "distorted, prejudicial and inconsistent with realities."

In urging the Council June 16 to extend the term of UNFICYP, Thant had warned that failure to do so could result in "an early resumption of fighting, which might well develop into heavy conflict." Thant said that contributory nations had agreed to keep their troops in UNFICYP for another 3 months. Thant estimated the cost of the 3-month extension at $7,300,000. (The U.S. already had pledged $2 million, Britain $1 million.) Thant said consolidation of Greek and Turkish Cypriot military positions in Nicosia and its suburbs had made it easier for both sides "to undertake operations in the future." Thant expressed pessimism over the "likelihood of a political solution in the immediate future." He said: "There is a misgiving on the part of the [Cypriot] government that the present situation may be frozen in a manner contrary to its political aims and also contrary to its aim to regain control over the whole island. It is feared that in the attempt to restore law, order and normality, violence and fighting may again break out."

Thant's discouragement about the political situation was based on a report June 13 from UN mediator Sakari S. Tuomioja, who, according to Thant, had offered no hope for an early solution. Thant said UNFICYP was "entitled to try to check" the "illegal" smuggling of arms into Cyprus by Greek and Turkish Cypriots. He said UNFICYP's ability to do so would determine the ability of the UN's "effort in Cyprus to succeed."

A UN spokesman June 25 announced a British decision to reduce the number of Britain's 1,800 troops in UNFICYP by 1,100-1,200 men. The planned reduction was coupled with a British agreement to continue to contribute soldiers to UNFICYP in response to Thant's June 20 appeal. Australia, Denmark, Ireland, Finland and Sweden already had pledged continued contributions to UNFICYP. (The Greek Cypriot-controlled House of Representatives July 23 adopted a resolution calling for the withdrawal of the 1,000 British troops from UNFICYP. British Foreign Secy. R. A. Butler told the House of Commons July 27 that Britain would under no conditions give up its military bases in Cyprus.)

Kutchuk July 2 levelled charges of anti-Turkish Cypriot bias at "senior" UN officials in Cyprus and at Thant's June 16 report to the Security Council. Kutchuk singled out a suggestion by Thant that Turkey's 650 soldiers in Cyprus (under the 1959 Treaty of Alliance) return to their Nicosia barracks in compliance with Greek Cypriot demands. Asserting that the Turkish troops had moved into field positions because they had been in a Greek Cypriot area, Kutchuk said "it is ridiculous to impute responsibility to Turkey and the Turkish army contingent in adopting an unhelpful attitude adopted by Greece and the Greek army contingent which has actually taken part in the fighting on the island." Kutchuk said a "serious omission" in Thant's report was his failure to cite "the extremely destructive role Greece has played in the whole conflict in Cyprus." "From the very beginning," Kutchuk declared, "Greek army personnel have been sent to Cyprus in the hundreds and the Greek government has given full moral and material support to the Greek Cypriot leadership's unlawful and unconstitutional activities."

Replying July 3, Thant said Kutchuk's "charges, allegations and insinuations... unmistakably impugn the objectivity, integrity and good faith of senior members of the UN Secretariat in Cyprus."

The UN command in Nicosia July 4 advanced a plan to enforce a neutral zone at the "green" truce line set up in Nicosia. UN forces would be given the right to arrest, search, and "implicitly to disarm" anyone within 100 yards of each side of the line dividing the Greek and Turkish Cypriot communities. Galo Plaza Lasso, special UN representative in Cyprus, announced July 7 that such a free zone would be established.

Johnson Seeks to Mediate

Pres. Johnson, acting as a top-level mediator in the Cyprus dispute, held separate meetings in Washington with Turkish Premier Ismet Inonu June 22-23, 1964 and Greek Premier George Papandreou June 24-25. Mr. Johnson had initiated the discussions. His mediation efforts were aimed at bringing about direct Turkish-Greek negotiations over Cyprus to avert war between those 2 countries.

A joint communiqué issued at the conclusion of the Johnson-Inonu talks June 23 said the 2 leaders had: (a) Stressed the validity of the 1959 treaties that had established Cyprus' independence. (b) Discussed "ways in which present difficulties might be adjusted by negotiation and agreement" and emphasized "the urgent necessity for such agreements." (c) "Considered ways in which their countries could strengthen the efforts of the UN with respect to the safety and security of the communities in Cyprus." (d) "Strengthened the broad understanding already existing between Turkey and the U.S."

Inonu conferred with UN Secy. Gen. U Thant at UN headquarters in New York June 24. Inonu was said to have informed Thant of "the gist of his talk" with Pres. Johnson, and he and Thant discussed "important aspects of the Cyprus problem." Inonu said at a news conference in New York June 25 that "sooner or later the United States will have to take a stand" if the Cyprus crisis was to be solved. Inonu said he favored direct negotiations between Greece and Turkey.

A joint communique issued at the conclusion of the Johnson-Papandreou talks June 25 merely said that the 2 leaders had had "a sincere and useful exchange of views on the Cyprus situation" and that "both expressed full support of the efforts undertaken by the Security Council and the Secretary General of the UN for the establishment of peace in the island and for rapidly finding a permanent solution." After the talks Papandreou issued a statement that, in effect, rejected the U.S.' mediation efforts. Papandreou said: "No one is more competent than the United Nations mediator" to conduct the negotiations; "so long as there is a [UN] mediator I do not see what services other people could offer"; the 1959 Cyprus pacts were no longer valid, and the Cypriots should be allowed to determine their future by plebiscite.

Papandreou met with Secy. Gen. Thant at UN headquarters in New York June 26 and reiterated his arguments for self-determination. At a news conference earlier that day, Papandreou had said his refusal to engage in direct talks with Turkey was based on the belief that in the current situation it would be "not a conversation but 2 monologues, 2 deaf men talking about different things." Papandreou also conferred with U.S. State Undersecy. George W. Ball June 26, and Thant discussed the Cyprus situation with Ball and Sakari S. Tuomioja, UN mediator for Cyprus.

Thant and UN Undersecy. (for political affairs) Ralph Bunche met on the Cyprus situation June 27 with U.S. Amb. Adlai Stevenson, his deputy, Charles W. Yost, and U.S. Asst. State Secy. Harlan Cleveland. Cleveland said later that the threat of war over Cyprus was "getting greater, not less." Warning that Cyprus "could sink under the weight of armaments," Cleveland emphasized the need to reconcile Greek and Turkish Cypriot differences.

Inonu left the U.S. June 26 and arrived in London June 27 for talks with British Prime Min. Sir Alec Douglas-Home. A communique issued after a 2-hour discussion June 29 said the 2 leaders (a) had agreed that the 1959 Cyprus treaty was still valid and (b) had "considered ways of strengthening" UN peace efforts in Cyprus. Inonu was reported June 30 to have told Douglas-Home that Turkey's price for agreeing to *enosis* (Cyprus' proposed union with Greece) was partition of the island, exchange of the Greek and Turkish Cypriot populations and union of the Turkish portion of Cyprus with Turkey.

Papandreou went to Paris after leaving the U.S. and conferred with French Pres. Charles de Gaulle June 29. Papandreou said after the meeting that de Gaulle had displayed "full understanding" of the Cyprus situation. Papandreou said at a news conference June 30 that Greece would welcome efforts by France "to exert a moral influence... to reach a solution of the Cyprus problem." (Papandreou June 30 had rejected a British offer to visit London to discuss Cyprus July 1 and 2.)

U.S. Undersecy. Ball had paved the way for Pres. Johnson's mediation efforts with visits to Athens June 10 and Ankara June 11. Following a meeting with Ball, Papandreou said June 10 that he had received from Ball Mr. Johnson's reply to a message he had sent the President June 5 on reports of a threatened Turkish invasion of Cyprus. Papandreou said: "I told the President that such action might have grave consequences." After conferring with Inonu June 11, Ball said (according to a Turkish communique): The U.S. "believes that any solution to the Cyprus question must be in the interest of Turkey and Greece and ... that a solution must be found in the shortest time possible." Ball returned to Washington June 12 and reported to Pres. Johnson. Ball said later that he had told Greek and Turkish officials that war between them was "unthinkable." Ball, who had visited Greece, Turkey and Cyprus in February, said the Cyprus situation remained "dangerous." But he said that since February there had been a "developing awareness" of the need to settle the problem peacefully.

Grivas Returns

Gen. George Grivas, who had led Greek Cypriot resistance during the British occupation of the island, arrived in Cyprus June 12, 1964. A Greek government spokesman in Athens said June 22 that Grivas, who had not been in Cyprus since 1959, had returned from Athens on his own initiative, as a private citizen, to help restore peace. But a Cyprus government spokesman indicated June 22 that Grivas was in Cyprus "in an advisory capacity on military questions" and that he already had met with Pres. Makarios and other Cyprus officials.

Grivas said June 24 that Cyprus' political future should be decided by a referendum that should be held "within the shortest possible period." In his first public statement since returning to Cyprus, Grivas declared in a broadcast in Nicosia that "any other solution is unjust and unacceptable." Grivas, who favored *enosis* (Cyprus' union with Greece), warned that "a compromise solution" would only result in fresh "destructive conflagrations."

Grivas reiterated his demands for a referendum in a speech to a crowd of about 10,000 persons in Nicosia June 28. He urged his listeners to "march hand in hand toward victory or glorious death" in the fight for a "free Cyprus." Defending his right to return to the island, Grivas said: "I have not come here as a politician. ... I have come as a national leader. I have extended a hand to everybody, and I am collaborating with Archbishop Makarios in perfect harmony." Offering friendship for Turkish Cypriots, Grivas said they could return to their homes safely, including those who were armed.

Cypriot Vice Pres. Kutchuk June 29 called Grivas' offer of friendship an "empty offer" of "bait." Kutchuk had challenged Grivas' return to Cyprus June 24 in a cablegram to UN Secy. Gen. U Thant. Suggesting that Grivas' return was in contradiction to the UN Security Council's March resolutions on Cyprus, Kutchuk said it was "an act likely to worsen the situation." Charging that Grivas had "been responsible for the murder of hundreds of innocent lives," Kutchuk said the former resistance leader's plan was to "eliminate the Cypriot Turks and thus pave the way for union of Cyprus with Greece."

A statement issued by the UN command in Nicosia June 25 said: "It is our hope that his [Grivas'] presence here will help in the easing of the situation."

Grivas July 3 made his first public appeal for *enosis* since his return to Cyprus. Speaking to Nicosia hospital staff members and patients, Grivas said: "Our main aim is *enosis*" as the final solution to the Cyprus question; Cyprus would accept aid "from any quarter that offers it" to achieve *enosis*. Rauf Denktash, president of the Turkish Communal Chamber in Cyprus, said in a telegram to U Thant July 3 that Grivas had "confirmed by his statement today that the cause of the bloodshed in Cyprus is due to the Greek *enosis* campaign."

Starting a political tour of Cyprus, Grivas again appealed for *enosis* in a speech in Famagusta July 5. Grivas said: "I will fight to the end to achieve *enosis*"; "there will be enemies against this purpose, but what I want you to remember is Thermopylae and Marathon and the spilling of blood for one's freedom." Grivas spoke at swearing-in ceremonies for a newly-formed Greek Cypriot National Guard unit; Pres. Makarios, who favored independence for Cyprus rather than *enosis*, did not attend.

In a speech to the Cypriot House of Representatives July 6, Grivas said: "The tactics of our struggle for *enosis* must follow peaceful means"; "there are international organizations whose aim is to settle differences peacefully"; the *enosis* campaign should be based on self-determination and achieved by working largely through the UN.

Grivas was appointed commander of the Cyprus National Guard Aug. 13. He replaced Lt. Gen. George Karayannis, who had resigned that day, reportedly because of disagreements with Grivas. In addition to the guard command, Grivas also was given complete control over Cyprus's security forces.

Greek & Turkish Troop Landings

Evidence of clandestine landings of both Greek and Turkish troops on Cyprus added to the tense atmosphere on the island during July 1964. Greek and Turkish officials confirmed reports that their troops were landing in Cyprus, but each claimed the other had provoked such action by sending in troops first. A Turkish Foreign Ministry spokesman admitted July 11 that Turkey had been smuggling men and arms into Cyprus. (But on July 22 Turkey formally denied at the UN that it had sent to Cyprus any troops or arms except those allowed by treaty.) Greek Premier George Papandreou acknowledged July 21 that "there is no doubt that Cypriot volunteers, Cypriot students in Greece and deserters from the Greek army have personally appeared [in Cyprus]."

A UN spokesman in Nicosia said July 11 that Greece had landed 3,000 more troops than was legally permitted and that Turkey had sent 500 more than its legal garrison limit. Reports reaching Washington July 10 indicated that as many as 4,000 Greek troops and a smaller number of Turkish troops had landed secretly in Cyprus. First reports received July 3 by U.S. officials in Washington had indicated that Greece and Turkey had both been infiltrating small numbers of troops into Cyprus for the past 2 months. Many Cyprus reports stressed that most of the "troops" landed were Cypriots who had gone abroad for military training and that few were believed to be regular soldiers.

The Cyprus government held an emergency session on the troop infiltrations July 11. It delivered to the Turkish embassy in Nicosia July 14 a protest warning that if the Turkish troops were not withdrawn soon, Cyprus would be forced to "deal with the situation." The note called the Turkish landings "aggression" and a "violation of the territorial integrity and and sovereignty" of the Cyprus republic. The Cyprus government July 15 issued decrees restricting the entry of various relief supplies for Turkish Cypriots and advising Greek Cypriot businessmen to stop selling "strategic materials" to Turkish Cypriots.

Premier Papandreou promised July 21 to restrain Greek troops on Cyprus if Turkey would pledge not to invade the island. Papandreou called the Greek infiltrations "an individual response to the Cypriots' appeal to reinforce them in their defense."

Pres. Johnson had been reported July 4 to have sent renewed appeals to Greece and Turkey to exchange views on the Cyprus crisis. The State Department announced July 4 that ex-State Secy. Dean Acheson would go to Geneva at Mr. Johnson's request to "provide assistance that may be appropriate in helping to resolve the Cyprus crisis."

UN Secy. Gen. U Thant appealed July 16 to the governments of Cyprus, Greece and Turkey and to the Turkish Cypriot community to "do all within their power to halt this perilous trend [arms buildup] and to reverse it before it leads to a major clash in Cyprus, with all the dangers that such a clash entails."

Denmark and Sweden warned July 17 that they would withdraw their UNFICYP forces if Greece and Turkey continued to ignore UN appeals to stop the troop infiltrations.

The UN command in Nicosia July 24 confirmed reports that clandestine truck convoys were operating from the port of Limassol. A spokesman said that a convoy of 30 Greek Cypriot trucks loaded with arms had been seen. Newsmen had reported convoys of 32, 106 and 36 trucks sent the previous week to the area of the Troodos Mountains, a Greek Cypriot stronghold. Many of these trucks were reported to have gone on to the Nicosia region. UNFICYP troops reportedly had been prevented by Greek Cypriots from checking the Limassol dock area. U Thant July 22 had sent a message to Cyprus Pres. Makarios expressing his "growing concern" about interference with UNFICYP freedom of movement.

UN & French Peace Roles Sought

Pres. Makarios declared in Nicosia July 27 that he no longer believed an "agreed solution" of the Cyprus crisis was possible. He urged that the entire Cyprus problem be placed before the forthcoming session of the UN General Assembly. Makarios deplored "the efforts . . . made by various quarters [presumably the U.S. and Britain] to find, or rather impose, a solution outside the framework of the United Nations." He said the "present acuteness" of the Cyprus problem made imperative an exchange of views with the Greek government. A Reuters dispatch from Moscow July 26 had quoted Makarios as having told a Tass correspondent in Cyprus that if the UN could not cope with the Cyprus situation "we shall have to use force, unfortunately."

Makarios flew to Athens July 27 and, after conferring with Greek officials, signed a communique reaffirming their "complete identity of views."

Turkish Premier Ismet Inonu had urged France July 1 to assume an active role in the Cyprus dispute. At a meeting with Pres. Charles de Gaulle in Paris, Inonu appealed to the French leader "to take a close interest" in the Cyprus controversy and, "if necessary, to use his authority to reach a solution." Inonu said at a news conference later that he and de Gaulle had agreed on the need to establish peace and security in Cyprus. Reiterating Turkish opposition to *enosis*, Inonu said he favored a federal plan under which Greek and Turkish Cypriots would be "separated physically with a central administration."

TURKISH AIR ATTACKS & AFTERMATH
AUG.-DEC. 1964

Turkey's threat of military intervention in Cyprus was finally carried out Aug. 7, 1964. Determined to protect Turkish Cypriots involved in fresh communal fighting, Turkey sent military planes to bomb and strafe Greek Cypriot positions. The air attacks killed at least 100 Greek Cypriots and wounded 200 before they were halted by a UN Security Council cease-fire Aug. 9. The truce also stopped ground fighting on the island. Turkey had come under strong international pressure to cease its aerial operations against Cyprus, and the Cypriot government had been subjected to similar demands to halt its military activities against the Turkish Cypriots.

Prior to the outbreak of the fighting, new mediation efforts had been started in Geneva in July in a search for a political solution. The discussions were conducted by UN political mediator Sakari S. Tuomioja and were attended by Greek and Turkish representatives and by ex-State Secy. Dean Acheson as an informal U.S. observer. The conference deadlocked over a plan, proposed by Acheson that called for union of Cyprus with Greece in exchange for a Turkish military base on the island to protect Turkish Cypriots. Greece and Turkey accepted the plan in principle but disagreed on means of implementing it. Cypriot Pres. Makarios, however, expressed outright opposition to ceding even one inch of Cyprus territory to Turkey.

The ending of the armed strife was quickly followed by another dispute. The Greek Cypriots were accused of failing to lift all economic restrictions imposed on the Turkish Cypriot community in July. Turkey threatened to use force to bring in all necessary supplies. Another source of friction between Cyprus and Turkey arose over the rotation of the Turkish garrison on the island as provided for under the 1960 independence treaties. Ankara asked Cyprus for permission to replace 335 men Aug. 31, but Makarios refused and warned that he would employ force to *prevent the landing of new Turkish troops. As a result of Makarios' threat, Turkey temporarily deferred action on troop rotation.*

The blockade and troop rotation controversies were resolved peacefully through UN intercession. Following UN Security Council discussion of the blockade, Turkey agreed not to supply the Turkish Cypriots, while Greece and Cyprus agreed to lift the economic curbs. Cyprus announced Oct. 26 that it would permit Turkey to relieve its garrison. The approval was linked to an agreement to allow UNFICYP to control the Nicosia-Kyrenia road.

Turkish Planes Attack Cyprus

Turkish warplanes attacked widespread targets in northwestern Cyprus with rockets, machineguns, cannon and incendiary bombs Aug. 7-9, 1964 in support of Turkish Cypriot forces under heavy assault by Greek Cypriots. At least 100 Greek Cypriots were killed and 200 wounded. The crisis abated as Turkey and Cyprus Aug. 10 accepted a UN Security Council cease-fire proposal.

The Turkish military intervention was precipitated by sharp fighting that had erupted Aug. 5 between Greek and Turkish Cypriots near the villages of Mansoura and Kokkina in the northwest. A Cyprus radio broadcast Aug. 6 said that Greek Cypriot forces that day had repelled Turkish Cypriot attacks on their positions near Mansoura and other nearby Turkish villages. The broadcast said 4 Greek Cypriots had been killed. It accused the Turkish Cypriots of using a beachhead in the area to land men, arms and supplies from Turkey. Greek Cypriot forces Aug. 7 advanced in the Kokkina section in an effort to wrest control of the beachhead.

A Cypriot government announcement Aug. 7 said 4 U.S.-built Turkish air force jet planes that day had machinegunned the town of Polis, west of Kokkina, and had struck an Italian freighter in the harbor. The government declared a state of alert. Turkish Deputy Premier Kemal Satir said Aug. 8 that the flight over Polis was meant as a warning, and a UN spokesman said the Turkish planes had not strafed Polis during the Aug. 7 flight but had fired rockets toward the sea. The Turkish cabinet warned Aug. 8 that Cyprus "may be bombed" unless the U.S. succeeded in finding a solution to the Cyprus question.

Turkish planes later Aug. 8 strafed Polis and the villages of Xeros and Pakhyammos. 24 Greek Cypriots were killed and at least 200 wounded, the Nicosia government reported. One of 3 planes that attacked Xeros was shot down by ground fire; the pilot, unhurt, was taken to Nicosia for questioning. A Greek Cypriot gunboat was strafed in Xeros harbor; 5 crewmen were killed and 13 wounded.

During the Turkish air attack, ground fighting between Greek and Turkish Cypriots continued. Turkish women and children were evacuated from Kokkina, Mansoura and Ayios Theodoros; Greek Cypriots later occupied the latter 2 villages.

A Turkish government announcement Aug. 8 described the air attacks as a "police action" ordered by Pres. Ismet Inonu and limited to preventing Greek Cypriots from advancing on Turkish Cypriot positions in the Tylliria Promontory area. The announcement added: "In view of the actions that the Greek Cypriot president, Makarios, has undertaken to annihilate Turkish Cypriots around the Mansoura area, we contacted the UN and our allies for putting an end to this action. But we could not obtain any results. Turkish air force jets are now cleaning up all Greek Cypriot military vehicles that are on their way to annihilate Turkish Cypriots."

A Turkish Foreign Office announcement the same day said Turkey's planes would continue "a permanent vigil over Cyprus from the air."

Turkish planes renewed their attacks on northwest Cyprus Aug. 9, when 64 jets attacked the villages of Polis, Khrysokhous, Limni, Yialia, Pakhyammos, Ayios Theodoros and Pamos. A Greek Cypriot official said that 2 Turkish destroyers, 4 miles off Mansoura, had shelled Greek Cypriot coastal towns. A Turkish official said Ankara had ordered the new air strikes because the Greek Cypriots "had renewed their attacks on our villages this morning."

Pres. Makarios warned Aug. 9 that Greek Cypriots would carry out full-scale attacks on Turkish Cypriot villages unless Turkey halted its air raids. Makarios said he had appealed for foreign medical aid for the air raid victims. He said he also had called on the USSR, Syria and the United Arab Republic (UAR) for military assistance. A reply by UAR Pres. Gamal Abdel Nasser, made public by Nicosia Aug. 11, said Nasser was ready to give Cyprus all the help it needed.

Makarios, in a message to Ankara Aug. 9, proposed to halt Greek Cypriot attacks on Turkish villages if Turkey stopped air raids first. Turkish Foreign Min. Feridun C. Erkin rejected the cease-fire suggestion. He insisted that Greek Cypriots would have to cease their military operations before Turkey called off its air strikes.

Turkey had informed the NATO military command Aug. 8 that it had withdrawn its air units and bases from NATO for use in the Cyprus crisis. Some Turkish army units had also been removed from NATO command for possible use in Cyprus. The NATO Council met on the Cyprus question Aug. 8, and NATO Secy. Gen. Manlio Brosio discussed the crisis Aug. 9 with the Greek and Turkish delegates. Brosio expressed concern in a letter to Pres. Inonu. Inonu said in reply Aug. 10: "Turkey does not wish to become involved in a war with Greece. We are persuaded that the ground for such a war does not exist. The 1960 treaty under which Turkey has assumed responsibility for the maintenance of constitutional order in Cyprus is also binding on Greece."

World Leaders Urge Peace

Greek Premier George Papandreou appealed to Makarios Aug. 8 to order Greek Cypriot "military operations" to "cease immediately." "The solution of the Cyprus problem," Papandreou said, "will be attained by peaceful means." An apparent reply by Makarios, broadcast by the Cyprus radio later Aug. 8, said Greek Cypriots were determined to fight "till death" to preserve their freedom. Papandreou, also directing his peace appeal to Turkey, said: "The Cyprus issue must be solved by peaceful means"; "Greece declares that in the case of Turkish aggression she will offer defense, which is both her right and duty." (Greek armed forces were alerted, and landing ships were prepared in Salonika and other Greek harbors for possible movement.)

Pres. Johnson Aug. 9 sent messages urging Cypriot, Greek and Turkish government officials to pursue peaceful means to settle the Cyprus dispute. The President urged the leaders of the 3 nations to permit the UN Security Council to continue in its efforts to find a solution to the dispute.

Soviet Premier Khrushchev sent messages to Inonu, Makarios and U Thant Aug. 9: Khrushchev urged Inonu to "stop military operations against" Cyprus Any move to solve the Cyprus problem by force, Khrushchev said, would "intensify the threat of war" in the Mediterranean. Khrushchev assured Makarios "of the sympathies of the Soviet people and government." (Khrushchev's letter to Makarios was in reply to a note, received Aug. 8, in which Makarios had informed him of attacks by Turkish planes and warships.) In his message to Thant, Khrushchev urged that the UN "take all possible steps for a peaceful settlement."

British Prime Min. Sir Alec Douglas-Home Aug. 10 praised the UN cease-fire resolution but said it was essential to seek "a lasting political settlement."

Inonu Aug. 11 also voiced a plea for a permanent solution. He did so in a letter to Greek Premier Papandreou. In reply to Papandreou's Aug. 9 note requesting a halt in the Turkish air attacks, Inonu said that "maintenance of friendly relations between our countries is the requirement of our national interests and ideals." Inonu stressed the need "to accelerate the Geneva talks [on Cyprus] and to come to an agreement as quickly as possible."

The Geneva talks, conducted by UN political mediator Sakari S. Tuomioja and attended by Greek and Turkish representatives and ex-State Secy. Dean Acheson as an informal U.S. observer, had reached an apparent impasse. Before returning to Cyprus July 30 after 3 days of talks with Greek officials in Athens, Makarios had said that Greece had rejected as "abso-

lutely unacceptable" Acheson's proposal for settling the dispute.
He said Acheson had proposed that (a) Cyprus unite with Greece,
(b) Turkish Cypriots retain and govern 2 enclaves on Cyprus,
(c) Greece turn over to Turkey the Dodecanese island of
Kastellorizo, (d) Turkey get a military base on Cyprus and
(e) Turkish Cypriots who left Cyprus be compensated. The U.S.
State Department said July 30 that the proposals mentioned by
Makarios had not been advanced as a formal "plan" and that
they were not necessarily submitted by Acheson. The department
said the Cyprus proposals cited by Makarios were the result of
private talks Acheson had held with Greek and Turkish delegates. The department assailed Makarios for attempting to sabotage the Geneva talks by premature disclosures.

Turkey & Cyprus Accept UN Truce

The Turkish air attacks on Cyprus and the accelerated
ground fighting on the island led to emergency meetings of the
UN Security Council Aug. 8-9. These meetings resulted in the
acceptance of the truce Aug. 10. The Cyprus government
reported Aug. 15 that 6 days of ground fighting in the
Mansoura-Kokkina region and the Turkish air attacks had cost
the lives of 53 Greek Cypriots — 25 soldiers and 28 civilians; 125
Greek Cypriots were wounded.

The Aug. 8 Security Council session had been requested by
Turkey and Cyprus:

●A complaint filed by Turkey with Council Pres. Sivert A.
Nielsen urged the Council "to consider the serious situation
created in Cyprus by the renewed and continuing attempts of the
Greek Cypriots to subdue by force of arms the Turkish community in Cyprus in order to perpetuate the usurpation of the
government by the Greek community."

●The Turkish request was followed by an appeal by Cyprus for a
Council meeting "in view of the deliberate unprovoked air armed
attacks against the unarmed civilians of Cyprus."

During Council debate Aug. 8, Cypriot delegate Zenon
Rossides said Turkey was threatening to invade Cyprus "within
the hour" with a force of 6 warships and 26 troop vessels. A com-

plaint of Turkish Cypriot Vice Pres. Fazil Kutchuk, read to the Council, charged that the Greek Cypriots had cut off Kitima's water supply and thereby were jeopardizing the lives of the town's 2,500 Turkish Cypriots.

The Council then adjourned but met in another emergency session Aug. 9 and approved by 9-0 vote (USSR and Czechoslovakia abstaining) a resolution calling on Turkey and Cyprus to observe an immediate cease-fire. The resolution, sponsored by U.S. Amb. Adlai E. Stevenson, urged Turkey "to cease instantly the bombardment... of... Cyprus" and called on Cyprus "to order the armed forces under its control to cease fire immediately." "All concerned" were asked "to cooperate fully with the UN commander [in Cyprus] in the restoration of peace and security." An amendment to the resolution (demanded by Cyprus, Greece, the USSR and Czechoslovakia) urged "all states to refrain from any action that might exacerbate the situation or contribute to the broadening of hostilities."

After the vote, Greek delegate Dimitri S. Bitsios warned that if the resolution "does not lead to any result," "then Greece will lend its assistance to Cyprus through the medium of its aviation and by all military means available to it."

The 2d emergency Council meeting had been called by Rossides following the renewed Turkish air raids on Cyprus.

Cyprus and Greece later Aug. 9 requested another Council session. They acted on reports that Turkey was landing troops in Cyprus, but Greece withdrew its request on determining that the reports were unfounded.

Turkey and Cyprus approved the Council's cease-fire resolution Aug. 10 although Turkey's acceptance, given in a message to Council Pres. Nielsen, was conditional. Asserting that Ankara "has decided to stop immediately the action of the Turkish aircraft over the Mansoura-Kokkina region," Turkish Pres. Inonu warned that Turkey's observance of the truce "will only make sense... if your appeal for a cease-fire is heeded by the Greek Cypriots." Inonu warned that Turkey would continue its "reconnaissance and warning flights" over Cyprus until the Greek Cypriot forces in the northwestern sector withdrew to positions they had held prior to Aug. 5.

In approving the truce, Pres. Makarios said in messages to UN Secy. Gen. U Thant and Nielsen that "we had unilaterally ordered a cease-fire in the evening of Saturday, Aug. 8."

Thant said Aug. 10 that Turkey's and Cyprus' acceptance of the cease-fire provided "an opportunity for definitively ending fighting and relaxing tension in Cyprus." Thant added that he would exert "every effort toward constructive peace-keeping arrangements in all areas of the island." Thant appealed to Greece, Turkey and the Greek and Turkish communities in Cyprus to cooperate with Gen. Kodendera S. Thimayya, commander of UNFICYP.

The UN Security Council reconvened Aug. 11 after receiving a request from the Nicosia regime that day to meet on its complaint that Turkish planes had flown over the island earlier Aug. 11 in a violation of the cease-fire agreement. After 3 hours of debate, the Council requested a halt to flights over Cyprus. The Council also ordered UNFICYP to increase its patrols in the Mansoura-Kokkina area. (UN troops had resumed patrols in that area Aug. 10, for the first time in 2 days, as sporadic clashes and Turkish air attacks in the section were reported.) In Council debate Aug. 11 Cypriot delegate Rossides had charged that Turkish jets had flown over Cyprus that day. Rossides said that prior to the acceptance of the truce, Turkish air attacks on northwest Cyprus Aug. 10 had resulted in 10 casualties and that Turkish warships had landed supplies at Kokkina Aug. 8. Turkish representative Orhan Eralp defended Turkey's reconnaissance flights on the ground that they were needed to determine Greek Cypriot military intentions in the Mansoura-Kokkina area. U.S. Amb. Stevenson and British delegate Sir Patrick Dean upheld this contention. Stevenson said Turkey would have no need to maintain the surveillance flights if the truce were observed.

Turkey agreed Aug. 12 to halt the reconnaissance flights over Cyprus. Foreign Min. Feridun C. Erkin said Ankara had accepted the Council's recommendation to facilitate the UN's task in keeping the peace. Inonu said Turkey was "going to be helpful to the UN peace-keeping force and the Security Council." The Turkish Foreign Ministry Aug. 12 admitted one surveillance mission over Cyprus that day but said it had been conducted before Ankara received the Council's request to halt such flights.

Erkin disclosed Aug. 13 that Ankara had informed its allies beforehand of Turkey's planned air attacks on northwest Cyprus Aug. 7-9. Asserting that "there was nothing they [the allies] could do to stop us," Erkin said Turkey was "sick and fed up at the action of the Greeks." U.S. Amb.-to-Turkey Raymond A. Hare reportedly had urged Turkey not to land troops in Cyprus. Hare's appeal was said to have been responsible for Ankara's decision to accept the UN Security Council's Aug. 9 cease-fire resolution and the Council's subsequent request for an end to Turkish reconnaissance flights over Cyprus.

The *N.Y. Times* reported Aug. 13 that the Greek Cypriot attacks launched in the northwest Mansoura-Kokkina region Aug. 5 were in violation of an agreement with the Greek government. Pres. Makarios was said to have met 2 weeks previously with Greek Premier George Papandreou and Gen. George Grivas; all 3 reportedly had agreed that no military action would be taken against the Turkish Cypriots unless Athens was consulted beforehand and approved. Makarios and his associates reportedly had planned the attack in the Mansoura region in July to eliminate what they regarded as a potential landing point for a Turkish invasion. Papandreou was said to have assailed Makarios for the Mansoura offensive in a letter sent to the Cyprus president Aug. 11. The *Times* said that Cypriot Foreign Min. Spyros A. Kyprianou had met with Papandreou Aug. 11 and conveyed Makarios' indignation at Greece's failure to intervene militarily on Cyprus' side during the Turkish air attacks. Greece had confined its action in the crisis to sending 5 planes over Cyprus Aug. 9, as a "warning," but only after Turkey's 3d and most devastating air attack on Cyprus that day. Kyprianou conferred with Greek officials in Athens later and said on his return to Nicosia Aug. 17 that Greece had promised to assist Cyprus "with all forces" if Turkey attacked the island.

A UN force of 150 soldiers Aug. 20, 1964 dismantled 3 Turkish Cypriot gun positions near the Nicosia truce line separating the Turkish and Greek Cypriot communities. The Turkish Cypriots protested the demolition. A UN spokesman said the operation had been ordered earlier Aug. 20 following 2 weeks of fruitless negotiations by the UN with the Turkish Cypriots for the removal of the fortifications. According to a UN official, the demolition of the gun positions was necessary because they were a potential threat to UNFICYP's Nicosia Military Zone Command buildings. UNFICYP staged a show of force in Nicosia Aug. 21 in an effort to assert authority in the area and prevent a possible renewal of communal clashes. A newly formed mobile battle force of scout cars, armored vehicles and jeeps maneuvered about the city's northern suburbs in full view of Turkish Cypriot gun positions. The force sped about the Nicosia truce line Aug. 22.

The truce was breached twice Aug. 21; a Greek Cypriot was killed and a Turkish Cypriot policeman was seriously wounded in 2 separate shooting incidents near Paphos. Cyprus' air space in the northwest had been violated twice that day by unidentified planes, according to a Greek Cypriot spokesman. Greece had charged Aug. 20 that 2 Turkish planes had flown over the Greek islands of Samos and Rhodes Aug. 19. Athens protested in notes to NATO, the UN and Turkey.

USSR Vows to 'Defend' Cyprus

The Soviet Union promised Cyprus Aug. 15, 1964 that it would "defend" the island's "freedom and independence from a foreign invasion." The Russian statement, published by Tass, said Moscow was "prepared to begin negotiations on this matter right now." The statement was in reply to an appeal by Makarios to Moscow Aug. 9 for military assistance.

Soviet Premier Khrushchev charged Aug. 16 that Turkey's Aug. 7-9 air attacks on Cyprus had been part of a U.S.-British "imperialist plot" aimed at the Cyprus government. Speaking at Frunze, Kirghizia, Khrushchev warned Turkey that the USSR could "not remain indifferent to the threat of an armed conflict" near the Soviet Union's southern frontier.

Britain appealed to the Soviet Union Aug. 17 to "conform" to the UN Security Council's Aug. 9 resolutions, "which called on all states to refrain from any action that might exacerbate the situation in Cyprus and broaden hostilities." The U.S. State Department Aug. 17 also cited the necessity of upholding the Council resolution in a statement scoffing at Khrushchev's charges of a U.S.-British "imperialist plot."

Turkish Foreign Min. Erkin said Aug. 17 that the Soviet pledge of aid to Cyprus "introduces a new and important element in the Cyprus crisis." Erkin warned Aug. 19 that "if there is a danger of war" over Cyprus and "if Russia sends military aid to Cyprus," Turkey "might close" the strategic Bosporus Straits to Soviet ships. Erkin's statement was in response to a question about a Soviet freighter reportedly carrying military supplies to Cyprus.

Tass Aug. 19 quoted Makarios as having thanked Khrushchev for his pledge to aid Cyprus. Makarios had said: "With the mighty support of your great country, the people of Cyprus believe that their just struggle for full independence... will be completed successfully"; "your unequivocal warning to the aggressor is an invaluable contribution to the international peace." Possible Soviet aid to Cyprus reportedly was the subject of a conference Makarios held with Soviet Amb. Pavel K. Yermoshin in Nicosia Aug. 22. The talks were attended by Foreign Min. Kyprianou.

Greece & Turkey Return Troops to NATO

Greece and Turkey agreed Aug. 19 to return to NATO command the military units they had withdrawn during the height of the crisis the previous week. The decision followed appeals to both governments by NATO Secy. Gen. Manlio Brosio and Gen. Lyman L. Lemnitzer, supreme Allied commander in Europe. Turkey had withdrawn its air units and some bases from NATO command Aug. 8 for possible use in Cyprus. Greece had decided Aug. 17 to take some of its army, navy and air units from NATO "to fulfill her [Greece's] commitments toward Cyprus to support it against any Turkish attack." The Athens statement said Greece had protested to Gen. Lemnitzer about Turkey's NATO withdrawals, "but its protest had remained unanswered." Greek and Turkish troops and equipment had remained at their

NATO bases although transferred to their respective national commands. The only personnel withdrawn involved the shift of Greek representatives from NATO's Southeastern Europe headquarters in Izmir, Turkey to Salonika, Greece.

Dispute over Blockade

The Aug. 9 truce halting the fighting in Cyprus was threatened by a new dispute between the Greek and Turkish Cypriots. The Cyprus government announced Aug. 19 the lifting of an economic blockade of Turkish Cypriot communities that it had imposed in July following reports of Turkish troop landings. The Turkish Cypriots, however, charged that not all the economic restrictions had been removed. The tenuous cease-fire was further imperiled by a Turkish government threat to use force to bring in supplies to the Turkish Cypriots. UN intervention followed by Greek Cypriot agreement to withdraw all economic barriers finally led to a resolution of the crisis in September.

Vice Pres. Fazil Kutchuk had warned Pres. Makarios Aug 13 that if he did not "want the blood to flow again he must lift the economic blockade." Turkey warned Greece Aug. 13 that Turkey would resume warplane flights over Cyprus unless the blockade were lifted. Turkey appealed to the U.S., Sweden, Britain, Greece and Denmark Aug. 15 to help ease the economic hardships of Turkish Cypriots.

The blockade was ended under an agreement that UN authorities in Nicosia negotiated Aug. 18 with the Cyprus government. A UN communique said the elimination of the "severe economic restrictions" would not prejudice "the normal military security measures that are inevitable in view of the present circumstances." The communique said the International Red Cross would conduct relief operations "with the full backing and assistance" of UNFICYP.

Paphos, the hardest hit of Turkish communities on the southwest coast, began to receive its normal water supply Aug. 19, and the UN reported that fruit and vegetables were being made available to the village's Turks. Economic restrictions were ,eased in Nicosia as the Turkish quarter received 2,300 gallons of gasoline. The food, fuel and water blockade was also lifted in the hard-pressed northwest Turkish communities of Polis, Kokkina, Lefka and Limnitis.

Gen. Kodendera S. Thimayya, UNFICYP commander, and UN mediator Galo Plaza Lasso met with Makarios Aug. 20 to discuss the lifting of the remainder of the economic blockade restrictions. The Turkish Cypriots had complained that, despite Nicosia's acceptance of the UN plan, food shipments to some communities were still being held up. Kokkina in the northwest suffered most among the Turkish communities. The Greek Cypriots refused to let emergency supplies enter Kokkina Aug. 21, but they permitted some food shipments into the village Aug. 22. A Turkish Cypriot spokesman said Greek Cypriot security forces in Nicosia barred milk shipments to children in the city's Turkish quarter. Kutchuk charged in a protest to Thimayya Aug. 24 that "the number of Turkish Cypriot villages faced with imminent starvation is increasing every day." Kutchuk was said to have told Thimayya that the Turkish army's 650-man contingent on the island had been deprived of food and kerosene.

In a note to UN Security Council Pres. Sivert Nielsen, Turkey protested Aug. 26 about Cyprus' alleged refusal to observe the UN agreement to lift the economic blockade. Turkey said it might seek an emergency Council meeting "to discuss and remedy the explosive situation created by the illegal 'blockade' of the unlawful Greek Cypriot government."

Geneva Talks

Greek and Turkish representatives returned to Geneva Aug. 14 to resume discussions with UN mediator Sakari S. Tuomioja and Dean Acheson. But the talks were interrupted when Tuomioja suffered a stroke Aug. 16. UN Secy. Gen. U Thant temporarily replaced Tuomioja with Pier Spinelli, UN representative in Europe. Spinelli, who was on a UN mission in Yemen, arrived in Geneva Aug. 19 for the talks. Tuomioja died Sept. 9. Galo Plaza Lasso succeeded him Sept. 17 but retained his other post as Thant's special representative in Cyprus.

Prof. Nihat Erim, Turkish representative at the Geneva talks, said Aug. 19 that he had accepted Acheson's proposals on Cyprus "as a basis of discussion." (The reported Acheson proposals called for Cyprus' union with Greece and concessions to Turkey.)

In a note to Turkish Premier Inonu Aug. 13, Greek Premier George Papandreou had said that Athens would help Tuomioja in "reaching an agreed solution" at the Geneva conference. Papandreou said if the Geneva talks collapsed, the remaining alternative would be "recourse" to the UN General Assembly. Papandreou's note was in reply to an Aug. 11 Inonu message suggesting that the 2 leaders seek a permanent solution to the Cyprus dispute.

The Geneva talks were resumed after the replacement of the mediator but were halted again after the issuance Aug. 25 of a joint communique in which Papandreou and Makarios insisted that the Cyprus question be placed before the UN General Assembly at its next session (in November). In a statement made in Nicosia Aug. 25 after returning from an all-day conference with Greek officials in Athens, Makarios assailed the Geneva talks and said that "the efforts that have been exerted to remove the Cyprus question from its right basis have completely failed." Prior to leaving for Athens, Makarios had said that he was going to the Greek capital to "finally denounce the Acheson plan." Makarios said his government "would not give even the smallest plot of land in Cyprus to the Turks." (The Acheson plan had also been attacked Aug. 23 by Cyprus House of Representatives Pres. Glafkos Clerides. "If union with Greece is to take place first and then Greece is to negotiate with Turkey what the rights of the Turkish community in Cyprus are going to be and whether there will be a Turkish or NATO base in Cyprus, then this is an unacceptable proposition," Clerides said. He insisted that Cyprus "be freed from all the treaties [the 1960 pacts which granted its freedom] and have complete independence.")

Commenting on the negotiations, U Thant said in Geneva Sept. 1 that "an agreed solution, at least for the moment, is out of the question." Thant said further discussions should include Cyprus, as well as Greece and Turkey.

Acheson returned to Washington Sept. 4 to report to Pres. Johnson. In an airport statement, Acheson asserted that the situation on the island had reached a point where "war could break out in 25 minutes." Denying that the Geneva talks had failed, Acheson said, "We...have greatly removed the differences between Greece and Turkey." He explained that a recess had been taken "to see...where we are going from here." Acheson assailed Makarios' role in the Cyprus talks, charging that "he threw monkey wrenches into the machinery."

Greece and Turkey were said to have deadlocked in Geneva on implementation of Acheson's plan for Cyprus, which previously they had accepted in principle: Both nations had favored Acheson's purported proposal to unite Cyprus with Greece in return for a Turkish military base on the island for the protection of the Turkish Cypriot minority; Greece, however, rejected Ankara's demand for an 800-square-mile garrison area on the ground that it was too large (1/5 the size of Cyprus) and was, therefore, tantamount to partition. Turkey insisted that the proposed base be situated on the coast for free access; Athens opposed this location for fear it could be used as a disembarkation point for a possible Turkish invasion. Turkey wanted sovereignty over the base, but Greece contended it should only be leased. Greece also rejected an Ankara demand that, after Cyprus' union with Greece, a Turkish deputy governor be appointed to protect the rights of Turkish Cypriots.

Acheson reported to Pres. Johnson Sept. 8. After the meeting, U.S. officials gave this assessment of the Cyprus crisis: Greece could help pacify the opposing parties and prevent a possible Mediterranean war by persuading Cyprus (a) to demobilize its National Guard, (b) to lift the economic blockade of Turkish Cypriot villages and (c) to permit Turkey to rotate its troops on Cyprus. Otherwise, it was feared, Turkey might be provoked into military action. Turkey's 2d postponement of the rotation of its troops on Cyprus was due to expire Sept. 12 and was not an indefinite deferment, as had at first been believed.

Anti-U.S. Riots in Turkey

Turkish citizens engaged in violent anti-U.S. demonstrations in Ankara, Istanbul and Izmir Aug. 27-29, 1964. The demonstrators were angered by an Aug. 16 note in which Pres. Johnson had warned Premier Inonu that Ankara would lose all U.S. aid if Turkey used U.S. military equipment in any intervention in Cyprus. Johnson was said to have informed Inonu that Turkey could not count on NATO assistance if the USSR intervened on the side of Cyprus. The demonstrators were said to have been further angered over what they regarded as a display of anti-Turkish bias by the U.S. at the Geneva conference talks on Cyprus. (2,000 Greek Cypriots had marched in Limassol Aug. 26, denouncing U.S. and British action in the crisis.)

In the Ankara demonstrations Aug. 27, several hundred students gathered before the American embassy carrying anti-U.S. slogans. A student leader declared in a speech that "we are against American imperialists." A mob of about 10,000 persons, including armed forces officers, converged on the U.S. embassy again Aug. 28. A rock-throwing demonstrator shattered an embassy window, and 3 Americans were beaten as they attempted to photograph the demonstration. The rioters finally dispersed, but many of them later attacked the nearby Greek embassy, breaking most of its windows and damaging 2 cars of Greek officials. 10 persons were injured in a student-organized demonstration in front of the U.S. embassy Aug. 29. After being dispersed by police, the rioters marched on the Greek embassy, stoned the building and broke windows. Police and soldiers in Istanbul Aug. 29 turned back 10,000 marchers who were heading for the district housing foreign consulates.

The most violent riots Aug. 29 occurred in Izmir, where a crowd of 2,000-3,000 wrecked and looted the buildings and grounds at the International Trade Fair. The rioting started with an attack on the U.S. pavilion and quickly spread to the exhibits of the USSR, Britain, UAR and Bulgaria. The disturbance was finally brought under control by police, reinforced by soldiers. The unrest, however, spread later to other parts of Izmir and continued through the early hours of Aug. 30. A crowd of several hundred Turks gathered before the city's police station and demanded the release of those arrested the night before, but they were dispersed by fire hoses. 62 persons were ordered held for trial in connection with the Izmir rioting. (The Izmir fair was closed Aug. 30 but reopened Aug. 31. The U.S. and Soviet pavilions remained shut.) The Soviet pavilion was wrecked because of the demonstrators' belief that the USSR was supporting the Greek position in the Cyprus dispute. This was denied in a note delivered to the Ankara government Aug. 29 by Soviet Charge d'Affaires Aleksei Voronin. Voronin said his government was supporting all interested parties in their efforts to reach a peaceful solution. He said the USSR had appealed to the Cypriot government several times not to mistreat the Turkish Cypriot minority.

In a broadcast Aug. 30, Inonu appealed to Turks to refrain from violent protests. Asserting that the demonstrations had been touched off by rumors, Inonu said Turkey would not accept an unfavorable Cyprus solution at the Geneva negotiations.

Turkish Troop Rotation Dispute

The Turkish Foreign Ministry said Aug. 29 that Ankara would delay "for a short time" the rotation of part of its 650-man garrison in Cyprus (as provided for under the 1960 treaties of independence). Turkey's request to the Cyprus government for permission to replace 335 men Aug. 31 had been rejected by Pres. Makarios with the warning that military means would be used to prevent the landing of new troops from Turkey. Makarios was said to have informed UN and Western officials that his government could no longer permit new Turkish troops to enter Cyprus in view of Turkey's Aug. 7-9 air attacks on Cyprus. The Cyprus government also contended that Turkey no longer had the treaty right to station troops in Cyprus. Greece had appealed to Turkey Aug. 28 to delay troop rotation for a month in the hope that Makarios would relax his opposition during that period.

Turkey had said it was prepared to back up the proposed troop movement with air and sea cover. A Turkish official conceded Aug. 29 that Ankara had yielded to "pressure" by the U.S., Britain, Greece and UN Secy. Gen. U Thant to postpone the troop replacement to avoid a military clash. Thant had warned

Turkey earlier Aug. 29 that the landing of new Turkish troops on Cyprus could result in a conflict with "broad and very serious implications." Thant also appealed to Turkey to confine its Cyprus garrison troops to their barracks and not deploy them along the Kyrenia road, which linked Nicosia with the north coast.

Although the U.S. had cautioned Turkey against troop rotation, a Washington statement Aug. 28 had reaffirmed the treaty rights of Turkey, along with Britain and Greece, to maintain troops in Cyprus.

This was the 2d time Turkey had delayed the troop rotation; because of similar opposition by Makarios, Ankara had postponed the troop shift from the original date of Aug. 16.

Pres. Glafkos Clerides of the Cyprus House of Representatives, serving as acting president of Cyprus while Makarios was on a state visit to the UAR, declared Aug. 29 that "we have not asked" for deferment of the troop rotation "and our position remains the same." "If the postponement means we are supposed to agree to a rotation later, then it merely postpones the problem," Clerides said.

In a complaint filed with UN Secy. Gen. U Thant Aug. 28, Turkey charged that 200 "Greek army personnel in full uniform" had landed at Limassol about midnight Aug. 24. In a telegram dated Aug. 27 and made public Aug. 28, Cypriot Vice Pres. Kutchuk appealed to the UN to implement "immediate and effective steps to prevent any further landings."

The UN Aug. 30 charged violation of the truce by flights over Cyprus that day of a Greek air force plane and 2 Turkish jets. The Cyprus government said the Greek plane had flown blood plasma to Nicosia. On its way back to Athens, the government explained, the plane flew over Turkish positions on the northwest in a "test flight" after it developed engine trouble.

A charge that Cyprus was interfering with sealed Turkish diplomatic mail had been filed with U Thant Aug. 25 and made public Aug. 27. The protest note, delivered by Turkish representative Orhan Eralp, said that "one of the most recent and flagrant instances ... occurred when Greek Cypriot authorities attempted at the Nicosia airport to seize 4 diplomatic pouches and 4 diplomatic bags, which were being taken to the Turkish embassy." Eralp said the smaller pouches had been returned to Turkish authorities, but he was unsure about the other bags.

Makarios Visits Nasser

Cypriot Pres. Makarios visited UAR Pres. Gamal Abdel Nasser in Alexandria Aug. 29-31 to inform him of the critical Cyprus situation and to seek possible military and political support. At the conclusion of the talks, Nasser declared in a communique Aug. 31 that the UAR would provide "all possible assistance to the Cyprus government's efforts to defend its country against foreign intervention." Nasser also pledged "support for Cyprus' "struggle" for "independence, territorial integrity and the right of self-determination."

On his arrival Aug. 28, Makarios, accompanied by Foreign Min. Kyprianou, had said to Nasser in an airport statement that Turkey and "certain other countries, serving their own sinister interests, are trying to impose" an unfavorable solution on Cyprus. In his talks with Nasser Aug. 30, Makarios was quoted as having said that Greek Cypriots "want unity with Greece, not unity with NATO." After the conclusion of the talks, Makarios said at a news conference Aug. 31: Cyprus did "not want to have any foreign bases" — "Greek bases, Turkish bases, British bases, NATO bases, any bases. We want Cyprus demilitarized."

While in Egypt, Makarios implied that the U.S. and Britain were responsible for the Turkish raids on Cyprus Aug. 7-9. A Cairo report said that Makarios, replying to a shout from an audience he was addressing in Alexandria that the raid was the work of "the Anglo-Americans," had said: "I do not wish to deny this." Kyprianou Sept. 2 repeated the charge that Turkey's air attacks had been carried out "with the tolerance" of the U.S. and Britain. Kyprianou said that the U.S. and Britain had refused "even after the events to condemn this barbarous attack on a noncombatant population." The reiteration of the accusation was coupled with the rejection of a demand by U.S. Amb. Taylor G. Belcher that the Nicosia regime issue "an immediate public denial that such statements have the support of the president of the republic."

UN Meets on Blockade & Other Matters

The Cypriot economic blockade and other issues in the Cyprus dispute were the subject of a UN Security Council meeting Sept. 11, 1964. At the meeting Cypriot Foreign Min. Kyprianou protested Turkey's plan to send an armed convoy with supplies for the Turkish Cypriots. Asserting that Kokkina had adequate supplies, Kyprianou warned that Nicosia would regard any Turkish shipment without its consent an "act of aggression." A Turkish note delivered to UN Secy. Gen. U Thant Sept. 10, however, had charged that since Aug. 5 "all the Turkish Cypriot towns and villages have been under an absolute state of siege..., and food supplies and clothing have been curtailed by the Greek Cypriots."

The Council meeting had been called on requests from Greece Sept. 5 and Turkey Sept. 6:

●In a note Sept. 5 to Council Pres. Platon D. Morozov of the USSR, Greek delegate Dmitri S. Bitsios urged the Council to meet before Sept. 16, the expiration date of the 1930 treaty covering the treatment of Greeks living in Turkey. Bitsios accused Turkey of having taken "provocative measures" that "have culminated in the expulsion of Greek residents of Istanbul, which has taken on the character of mass deportation." Bitsios predicted that "these measures will be further intensified" when the treaty terminated. Bitsios complained that Athens' protests to Ankara and Thant to bring a stop to the expulsion of Greeks had been unavailing. According to Greek estimates, more than 1,000 of Istanbul's 12,000 Greeks had been expelled from Turkey since Dec. 1963, the start of the Cyprus crisis.

●Turkish delegate Orhan Eralp's Sept. 6 note to Morozov requesting a Council meeting charged that: (a) Greece had violated the demilitarization treaty for the Dodecanese Islands by shipping troops there. (b) Greece had deployed troops on Turkey's frontier in "western Thrace." (c) Greece had "invaded" Cyprus with military equipment in violation of Security Council resolutions. (d) Greece sought "to impose a solution by force to the Cyprus problem"; Athens had condoned "the massacres committed and inhuman measures of hunger and thirst taken by Greek Cypriots against the Turkish community in Cyprus."

The Security Council's meeting was followed by a Turkish government decision Sept. 14 to defer indefinitely plans to ship food and clothing to Kokkina. The shipment had been scheduled to leave Sept. 15, but Ankara delayed the move at the request of Thant, who feared that Turkey's action might provoke a clash with Cyprus. (UN helicopters had delivered 2 tons of food and fuel to Kokkina Sept. 13.)

Turkey postponed sending the relief supplies even though Cyprus Pres. Makarios, at meetings Sept. 12 and 14 with UN diplomat Galo Plaza Lasso and Gen. Kodendera S. Thimayya, UNFICYP commander, had dropped his opposition to the proposed shipments. Thimayya had toured the Kokkina region Sept. 12. He said he had found many of the Turkish Cypriots there living "in subnormal conditions." He reported that there was only a 4-day supply of rations and that "food has got to come in or they will starve."

In response to Ankara's announced plans to relieve the Kokkina blockade, Makarios had warned Sept. 11 that his armed forces would "resist with every means" any attempt by Turkish vessels to "approach the Cyprus coast without the permission" of the Nicosia government. Denying Ankara's charges that Cyprus was guilty of "inhuman measures against the Turks" on Cyprus, Makarios invited UN and International Red Cross officials and "even" the Turkish charge d'affaires to "visit Kokkina in order to verify the existing situation regarding food supplies to the area." Although some food had been getting through to Kokkina as a result of the Aug. 19 agreement to lift the Cypriot blockade, the supplies were strictly rationed and considered inadequate.

The shipment dispute also involved the question of whether relief supplies should be taxed as imports. Turkey had insisted that they should enter duty-free. But Cyprus Defense Min. Polykarpos Georghadjis declared Sept. 11 that Turkey must first receive Nicosia's consent to send the supplies and then pay import duties on them. Otherwise, he said, the Turkish shipment would be regarded as "a kind of invasion."

In announcing plans to send supplies to Kokkina, Turkish Premier Ismet Inonu had warned Sept. 10 that "any interference during the disembarkment of these supplies . . will be considered an attack and answered the same way."

The UN reported Sept. 10 that Cypriot roadblocks had been lifted that day to permit food to be sent into the Turkish sectors of Famagusta and Larnaca. Makarios had warned Sept. 7 that those 2 communities would be placed in the "restricted" category along with the Nicosia, Lefka and Kokkina ones.

Cyprus & Greece Agree to End Blockade

A Cypriot plan for the lifting of the economic blockade of Turkish Cypriot communities was agreed to by Pres. Makarios and Greek Premier Papandreou at a meeting in Athens Sept. 17. The basis for the agreement were measures Makarios had proposed Sept. 15 to end the island's communal unrest.

Papandreou said after the Athens talks that Greece and Cyprus had "a common policy of pacification" for Cyprus that would help pave the way for a final political solution through UN mediation efforts. Papandreou said Greece would not go to war with Turkey over the rotation of Ankara's troops in Cyprus. "These secondary problems," Papandreou said, "should be settled in a satisfactory manner." Papandreou disclosed that Greek support of Cyprus was not unqualified. He said Athens would come to the aid of the Nicosia regime only in the case of an "unprovoked attack." Previous Greek guarantees had omitted this qualification.

Makarios' peace plan, announced Sept. 15, called for: (a) Removing "any economic restrictions and ... allow[ing] any quantity of foodstuffs to be supplied to or purchased by the Turkish Cypriots through the normal channels and on a permit granted by the Cyprus government." (b) Removing "all the armed posts throughout Cyprus, provided that the Turkish leadership will do the same." (c) Providing financial aid to Turkish Cypriots "who have been compelled ... to abandon their homes and are desirous of being resettled, and to afford them any protection." (d) Granting "a general amnesty, so that any Turkish rebel who may be under criminal charges of offenses committed during the rebellion may be relieved of any fear of arrest and punishment." (e) Accepting UN proposals for "practical security measures" for the island, "provided that such measures do not affect the political solution of the problem."

Immediately following the acceptance of the Makarios plan, the Cyprus government granted Turkey permission to send emergency relief to Turkish Cypriots in the village of Kokkina. A Turkish supply ship arrived at Famagusta Sept. 17, and food and medical equipment were unloaded Sept. 19. The emergency supplies also were sent to the Turkish village of Ambelikou. A 4-truck UN convoy had brought 9 tons of Cypriot government food to Kokkina Sept. 15, but the villagers, some of whom were armed, refused the supplies and halted the trucks at a roadblock about one mile from the community. The villagers accepted 6 tons of UN-delivered Turkish food Sept. 16.

In a further move aimed at pacifying the island, UN authorities announced Oct. 22 that they had negotiated an agreement for UNFICYP control of the strategic Nicosia-Kyrenia road in exchange for rotation of about 1/2 of the Turkish army's troop garrison on the island. The agreement went into effect Oct. 26 as (a) the strategic 16-mile highway was taken over by UN troops and reopened to civilian traffic and (b) 339 Turkish troops simultaneously were permitted by the Cyprus government to land in Famagusta to relieve the Turkish garrison. The road had been held by Turkish army and Turkish Cypriot forces since the communal fighting erupted in Dec. 1963. Under UN jurisdiction, the road was to be barred to military traffic and used by civilians only. UN Secy. Gen. U Thant had announced Sept. 25 that UN and Turkish government negotiators had reached agreement. But subsequent opposition by Turkish Cypriot leaders, who had not been consulted in the talks, prevented the pact's implementation, and further negotiations were required. Rauf Denktash, Turkish Cypriot leader, had warned Oct. 11 that if Turkey relinquished control of the Nicosia-Kyrenia road, Ankara would have "given away" its "last point in Cyprus" and would have "nothing further to surrender." Makarios had insisted Sept. 29 that he would refuse to permit Turkish troop rotation if Turkey did not yield the road to UNFICYP.

Municipal Councils Replaced

The Cyprus parliament voted Nov. 28, 1964 to replace the separate Greek and Turkish Cypriot municipal councils in major towns with single councils. The bill provided for the eventual election of council members "because of the present exceptional circumstances." Councilmen and mayors for the time being were to be appointed by the Greek Cypriot-dominated government. The council measure was approved by the 22 Greek Cypriot parliament members. Turkish Cypriot members had boycotted the chamber since Dec. 1963.

Term of UN Force Re-Extended

The UN Security Council Dec. 18, 1964 unanimously approved a resolution extending UNFICYP's life for another 3 months until Mar. 26, 1965. In debate prior to the vote, Cypriot Foreign Min. Kyprianou had charged Turkish Cypriots with rebelling "on the directives of the Turkish government." He said their purpose was to "further the political aims of the Turkish government for partition" of Cyprus, "or what they prefer to call 'federation'." Turkish representative Orhan Eralp replied that federation was the opposite of partition. But he said federation could result in partition if Cyprus united with Greece. In a report to the Council Dec. 12, UN Secy. Gen. U Thant had estimated the cost of UNFICYP's operation for the next 3 months at $6,175,000 at the force's current strength of 6,279 men.

UNEASY PEACE & RENEWED VIOLENCE 1965-8

The UN's political and peace-keeping efforts maintained stability in Cyprus during 1965-7 despite threats of political and military upheaval. UNFICYP settled down as an apparently permanent fixture on the island as the UN Security Council periodically extended its term of service. A proposal for direct Turkish-Greek talks to find a solution to the dispute was proposed by Ankara Mar. 19, 1965. The talks were held in Sept. 1967 but failed to produce agreement. The negotiations reflected Turkey's growing concern about the alleged mistreatment of the Turkish Cypriot minority. UN representative Galo Plaza Lasso reported to U Thant Mar. 26, 1965 that his mediation efforts had failed.

Turkish Cypriot discontent was aroused further by new political restrictions imposed by the Greek Cypriot-dominated government. Electoral reforms approved by the legislature July 23, 1965 virtually dismissed Turkish Cypriot leader Fazil Kutchuk by not extending his term as vice president and replaced the separate Greek and Turkish Cypriot voting rolls with a common electoral roll. The Security Council debated this latest political crisis but took no definitive action. The political deterioration was coupled with an outbreak of fresh communal clashes and new threats of international repercussions. The reported shipment of Soviet missiles to Cyprus in Mar. 1965 for the defense of the Makarios government evoked a warning from Turkey that it would bomb the missile sites in Cyprus or the ships carrying the missiles to the island. The Cyprus dispute affected internal developments in the Greek government in Apr. 1966 when 2 cabinet officials, including the foreign minister, resigned. The resignations were prompted by the government's support of Cypriot Defense Min. Grivas in his feud with Makarios.

Turkey renewed its threat of military intervention in Nov. 1967 following the outbreak of a serious clash between Greek and Turkish Cypriots. The Ankara government backed its warning *by mobilizing its armed forces and thus posing the risk of war with Greece. The U.S., the UN and NATO sought to defuse the tense situation, and Greece and Turkey backed down from their warring posture in compliance with a UN Security Council call for restraint. A more permanent peace appeared to take hold as Greece and Turkey Dec. 3, 1967 signed a pact that included provisions for (a) the removal from Cyprus of all their troops not authorized under the 1960 independence accord and (b) the expansion of UNFICYP. The establishment of a Turkish Cypriot "transitional administration" Dec. 28, 1967 led to a breakdown in implementation of the Greek and Turkish troop withdrawal. Intercession by U Thant settled the dispute, and the soldiers were pulled out of Cyprus in Jan. 1968.*

Makarios was reelected to a 2d 5-year term in 1968. His first presidential term, which had expired in 1965, had been extended twice by the Greek Cypriot parliament because of the continued crisis.

Relative calm prevailed in Cyprus through 1968-9, but a permanent political solution to the Greek and Turkish Cypriot dispute appeared to be as elusive as ever.

USSR Proposes Federal Government

Soviet Foreign Min. Andrei Gromyko proposed Jan. 21, 1965 that the island's 2 "national communities" of Greek and Turkish Cypriots "choose a federal form" of government as a means of resolving the country's political impasse. Gromyko's suggestion appeared in the Soviet government newspaper *Izvestia*. Cypriot Foreign Min. Stavros Costopopoulos said Jan. 22 that Gromyko's proposal was unworkable because "the Turkish minority is spread out throughout the island, and nowhere is it a majority of the population." Pres. Makarios also opposed the proposal. (Makarios Jan. 3 had proposed a constitutional amendment to replace the separate Greek and Turkish voting rolls with a combined roll. Since Greek voters outnumbered Turkish voters 4 to 1, Makarios' proposal would diminish the chances of Turkish Cypriot election to the House of Representatives.)

UN Force Extended; New Strife Foreseen

The UN Security Council Mar. 19, 1965 unanimously approved a resolution extending the life of the 6,000-man UN peace-keeping force in Cyprus for another 3 months — from Mar. 26 through June 26. The cost of the force's operation for the 3 months was estimated at $6,425,000. UNFICYP's operating expenses for the first year until Mar. 26 would total $20,700,000.

UN Secy. Gen. U Thant had urged the Security Council Mar. 12 to approve the extension to cope with an increasing threat of new fighting between the Greek and Turkish Cypriot communities. In a report to the Council, Thant said that in the past 3 months the Cyprus government had received "an increased influx of various types of light and heavy military equipment." He said these supplies had been secretly brought in through the new port of Boghaz, 16 miles north of Famagusta, in violation of a Sept. 10, 1964 agreement requiring that Nicosia officials inform UN authorities of such deliveries. Thant said that the Turkish Cypriots also were expanding their arsenal of arms and that a renewal of communal clashes was "likely to be more severe than before." Thant's report was based on a firsthand account of the situation submitted to him Mar. 3 by Galo Plaza Lasso, the UN mediator in Cyprus. Plaza Lasso had said in Athens Feb. 27 that he had failed so far to find an "agreed solution" to the dispute because both sides had not "budged an inch from their extreme positions." Plaza Lasso had stopped in Athens *en route* from Nicosia to discuss the Cyprus problem with Greek government officials. Before returning to New York, he flew to London to confer with British officials.

Turkey's representative to the UN, Orhan Eralp, had charged in a letter to Thant Feb. 9 that the Greek Cypriots were preparing to attack the Turkish Cypriot community.

A counter-complaint filed with Thant Feb. 19 by Zenon Rossides, head of Cyprus' mission to the UN, stated that Eralp had been seeking to "create an atmosphere of tension and alarm" by false charges of Greek Cypriot military preparations. Rossides recalled that he had informed Thant Feb. 4 of "factual and incontrovertible evidence of preparation for attack against the state by Turkish Cypriot rebels."

Clashes in Lefka & Ambelikou

UNFICYP authorities reported Mar. 13 that Greek and Turkish Cypriots had exchanged gunfire Mar. 12 and 13 near the Turkish enclave of Lefka, 35 miles west of Nicosia. There were no casualties. An Ankara broadcast warned Mar. 14 that unless UNFICYP removed Greek Cypriot positions at Lefka, Turkey would be forced to intervene militarily. Pres. Makarios replied Mar. 15 that if Turkey invaded or bombed Cyprus, the Cypriot forces would "neutralize the pockets of the Turkish insurrection and face the attack from outside free from any internal distractions."

Greek Cypriot national guardsmen and Turkish Cypriots fought each other sporadically Mar. 15 and 16 in Ambelikou, near Lefka. One guardsman and one Turkish Cypriot were killed Mar. 15. The guardsmen had been sent to the Ambelikou-Lefka area Mar. 12 after Turkish Cypriots attempted to improve a road linking the 2 villages. Turkish Cypriot sources claimed that the Greek Cypriot force had isolated Ambelikou, causing a food shortage and cutting off Ambelikou's water supply.

In UN Security Council debate Mar. 17, U Thant reported that Gen. Kodendera S. Thimayya, UNFICYP commander, had met with Greek and Turkish Cypriots in the Lefka area. In a supplementary report on the incident, Thant indicated that the fighting had been precipitated by unwarranted Greek Cypriot suspicions that the Turkish Cypriots were erecting new fortified positions in the area. Thant suggested that the Greek Cypriots' retaliatory action in moving forces into the region and setting up military positions of their own was in violation of an agreement not to fortify the Lefka area. Orhan Eralp, Turkish delegate to the UN, charged that Greece was "perhaps the senior partner" in the "Greek Cypriot attempt to impose an impossible solution by force" in Cyprus. Asserting that Ankara opposed such a solution, Eralp warned that Turkey would intervene militarily to protect the rights of Turkish Cypriots. Cypriot Foreign Min. Spyros A.

Kyprianou, supported by Greek representative Dimitri S. Bitsios, replied that the communal fighting that had been raging intermittently on the island since Dec. 1963 resulted from a Turkish Cypriot "subversive movement" abetted by "agents of Ankara." In defense of the Lefka attack, Kyprianou said the Greek Cypriot action there had been designed to prevent a widening of a "pocket of subversion" held by "Turkish terrorists."

Turkey Proposes Talks with Greece

Turkey's new premier, Suat Hayri Urguplu, proposed Mar. 19, 1965 that representatives of Turkey and Greece meet to discuss ways to prevent a further deterioration of the Cyprus situation. In a message to George Drossos, ex-Greek minister in Ankara (the message was published by the Athens newspaper *Ethnos*), Urguplu suggested that: (a) the projected conference be held at any level desired by Athens, secretly or in public; (b) the talks be confined to ending hostilities in Cyprus and to normalizing Greek-Turkish relations, while negotiation of the island's political status be deferred; (c) Greece and Turkey refrain from taking any unilateral action in the dispute. Deploring the "inhuman" treatment to which, he said, the Turkish Cypriots were subjected, Urguplu said: "Let him [Pres. Makarios] fortify the island," but he "must secure" for the Turkish minority "elementary human conditions." The Turkish Cypriots were "without food, work and clothing. They are not even allowed to walk around. They keep asking us for help."

Following a meeting of the National Security Council later Mar. 19, Urguplu again warned Greece and the Greek Cypriots about the conditions of the Turkish Cypriots. Describing the Cyprus controversy as "a Turkish-Greek problem," Urguplu said Ankara was "determined to take the most effective decisions in this connection."

In reply to Urguplu's proposal for bilateral talks, Greek Premier George Papandreou said Mar. 20 that there already was a UN mediator trying to settle the Cyprus dispute (Galo Plaza Lasso), and "we must help him fulfill his mission." Papandreou said Athens' "policy is to preserve peace and seek a final Cyprus solution in conditions of peace. It would be gratifying if this were also to be the new Turkish government's policy."

Soviet Missiles Shipped to Cyprus?

U.S. government officials confirmed Mar. 19, 1965 that they had received intelligence information that the Cypriot regime had built emplacements for the imminent arrival of Soviet-made anti-aircraft missiles. The missiles and other related equipment, apparently contracted for under a Sept. 1964 Soviet-Cyprus arms agreement, reportedly were being shipped through the United Arab Republic. It was believed the UAR also had served as a transshipment station for 30 Soviet-built T-34 tanks that had been sent to Cyprus earlier in March.

Turkey was said to have warned that it would bomb the missile sites or the ships carrying the missiles. In view of this threat, the U.S. State Department Mar. 19 called on Greece and Turkey to convene a new conference on Cyprus before they became involved in a war with each other or before major communal clashes erupted on the island. The department statement said: "The importation of antiaircraft missiles into Cyprus and similar movements of arms could only serve to make the problem more hazardous and the solutions more difficult."

The pro-Greek government newspaper *To Vima* of Athens had reported Mar. 17 that Greek Cypriot military personnel were in the UAR and were receiving training in the use of the Soviet missiles that were stockpiled there. The newspaper's report said: U.S. officials had informed the Greek government during the weekend of Turkey's opposition to the landing of Soviet weapons in Cyprus. Greek officials assured the U.S. that the weapons came under the Soviet-Cyprus arms pact and that the men being trained in their use in the UAR were Greek Cypriot army "volunteers," not members of the Greek armed forces. The Athens regime rejected suggestions that it attempt to discourage Cyprus from accepting the Soviet arms; it held that the missiles were strictly for defensive purposes.

Pres. Makarios conceded Mar. 29 that "part of" Soviet-made anti-aircraft missile equipment was already in Cyprus. But he would not say whether the missiles themselves had arrived or whether he was merely referring to the weapons' auxiliary parts, such as radar target-tracking devices. Makarios reiterated that the Soviet missile equipment had been delivered under terms of the Sept. 1964 USSR-Cyprus arms pact. The installation of the missiles, Makarios insisted, was "justifiable as a means to defend the island."

The State Department disclosed Mar. 29 that a ship carrying Soviet-manufactured missiles from the UAR had reached Cyprus and then had returned to its Egyptian port the previous week. A department spokesman denied a report Mar. 28 in the Greek Cypriot newspaper *Tharros* that ships of the U.S. 6th Fleet Mar. 27 had forced a Greek freighter carrying the Soviet equipment to return to the UAR without unloading its cargo. The U.S. was said to have pressured Greece and Cyprus to reject acceptance of the missiles on the island in order not to provoke Turkey. State Secy. Dean Rusk Mar. 24 had conferred with Cypriot Foreign Min. Spyros A. Kyprianou and reportedly had expressed U.S. concern over the Soviet missiles. The Soviet Communist Party newspaper *Pravda* accused the U.S. Mar. 28 of attempting to prevent the Greek Cypriots from "strengthening their defense potential."

Turkish Foreign Min. Hasan Ishik had said Mar. 21: His government had "evidence that there is Soviet military material in Cyprus." But "we also know that there are British and American arms there. We do not accuse one side more than the other." "Arms which come through the Dardanelles are not more offensive than those which pass through . . . Gibraltar."

UN Mediator Proposes New Government

The establishment of a new Cyprus government was proposed by Galo Plaza Lasso in a report submitted to U Thant Mar. 26, 1965 and made public Mar. 30. Plaza also called for direct negotiations between the conflicting Greek Cypriot and Turkish Cypriot community leaders. In formally disclosing his failure to find a solution to the dispute, Plaza said the "purpose of mediation could not be further served by my continuing to hold separate consultations" with the 2 sides. The mediator, who had been holding such consultations with the island's leaders since Sept. 16, 1964, said he believed that direct talks between the Greek and Turkish Cypriots would "produce fruitful results in solving a crisis which endangers both the safety of its [Cyprus'] own population and the relationships of the countries most directly concerned — Cyprus itself and Greece and Turkey."

Although the UN mediator said he felt it was "not appropriate at this stage to set forth precise recommendations," he did express opposition to the idea of *enosis* — Cyprus' union with Greece — and the Turkish proposal for partition of the island into separate Greek and Turkish communities. *Enosis,* Plaza warned, would probably result in "a new outbreak of violence." "The opposition of the Greek Cypriots to . . . geographical separation is hardly less strong than the position of the Turkish Cypriots to the imposition of *enosis*," he said. Plaza added: "It is not a question of denying the right a of a political majority [the Greek Cypriots] to rule but a question of the need to avoid the excessive dominance of one presently distinctive community over another to an extent and in a manner likely to delay indefinitely the unity of the population." Plaza said that in the event that Greek and Turkish Cypriot leaders entered into direct talks and reached "agreement on all major issues . . . , and should it then be necessary to refer the terms of settlement to the people of Cyprus directly, I consider that it would be essential to put to the people the basic settlement as a whole." "They should be asked to accept or reject it as a single package, and not in its various parts," he declared.

Plaza disclosed that Pres. Makarios had indicated his acceptance of a proposal of a UN-appointed "commission with a staff of observers to be present in Cyprus for as long as necessary" to direct the incorporation of the Turkish Cypriots into normal community life. According to Plaza, Makarios also had favored "a general amnesty and provision for resettlement of Turkish Cypriots who wish to leave the island and for the rehabilitation of those who would remain."

Plaza's report was denounced by the Turkish Foreign Ministry Mar. 31 on the ground that the mediator had exceeded his authority by giving his personal views of the Cyprus crisis. The ministry's statement, handed to Thant by Turkish delegate-to-UN Orhan Eralp, demanded that Plaza's position as mediator "be considered terminated." Turkey reportedly felt that Plaza's task was merely to attempt to get both sides to reach agreement but to render no opinion on the controversy.

Thant Apr. 2 rejected Turkey's charges. He said he had "found nothing in the mediator's report which I could consider as going beyond or being in any other respect incompatible with the functions of the mediator as defined." In disclosing his receipt Apr. 1 of Turkey's complaint, Thant said it was up to the Security Council to determine whether Plaza had complied with its Mar. 4, 1964 resolution to "promote a peaceful solution" of the Cyprus problem.

Turkish Cypriot leaders Apr. 2 also assailed the mediator's report as favorable to the Greek Cypriots. Their formal statement said: "The report does not take into consideration the legal rights of the Turkish Cypriot community and Turkey." Plaza's remarks, the statement said, could be interpreted to mean "that the Greeks shelve their demand for *enosis* only for as long as the 'risk' of opposition from the Turkish Cypriot community and Turkey persists."

Following the Turkish rejection of Plaza's report, UN mediation of the Cyprus issue was suspended. But the UN General Assembly Dec. 18, by 47-5 vote (54 abstentions, 11 absent), approved a resolution to continue the UN mediation. Opposition to the resolution centered on its failure to mention the obligations to respect the treaties governing Cyprus, although the resolution did cite the sovereign rights of the country. U.S. delegate Charles W. Yost, who cast a negative vote, declared that ignoring recognition of existing treaty rights would only exacerbate the conflict between Cyprus' Greek and Turkish communities.

Thant disclosed Dec. 31 that Plaza had submitted his resignation as mediator. He quoted Plaza as saying that he was quitting the post "in the interest of ... efforts to find a solution" to the communal dispute. Plaza was replaced, by Carlos A.

Bernardes of Brazil. Makarios contended Dec. 31 that Plaza had resigned because of Turkey's "unreasonable refusal to negotiate." Makarios said his government was opposed to the appointment of a new mediator.

Turkey Threatens to Deport Greeks

The Turkish government announced Apr. 19, 1965 that it planned to expel the remaining Greek citizens in Turkey and to "control" and possibly deport the Greek Orthodox Ecumenical Patriarchate in Istanbul. The Patriarchate was headed by Athenagoras I, spiritual leader of the Christian Orthodox Church. (The Turkish regime, however, never did go through with its threat to expel the Greeks.)

Ankara's threats, announced by Interior Min. Ismail Hakki Akbogan, reportedly were aimed at pressuring Greece in its current informal talks with Turkey on the Cyprus dispute. Greek Foreign Min. Stavros Costopoulos, who had been participating in these discussions in Athens for the previous 5 weeks with Turkish Amb. Turan Tuluy, reportedly informed Tuluy Apr. 21 that he was suspending the conferences in view of the Turkish threats.

About 9,000 Greeks had been deported or had left Turkey voluntarily since Ankara's Sept. 16, 1964 abrogation of the Turkish-Greek treaty recognizing Greek residence rights in Turkey. The remaining Greeks subject to the new expulsion order numbered 2,875, according to the Turkish Interior Ministry.

The "control" order governing the Ecumenical Patriarchate went into effect Apr. 22 as Turkish officials began an examination of its finances. Ankara's action followed Turkish newspaper charges that Athenagoras, a Turkish subject, had refused to permit government auditors to inspect the Patriarchate's financial books. A Patriarchate spokesman denied the charges.

In a retaliatory move, Athens Apr. 24 announced the temporary suspension of a Greek-Turkish agreement that had provided for reciprocal abolition of consular visas. Hereafter, Turks entering Greece would be required to obtain visas. Ankara had enforced a similar measure on Greek visitors to Turkey in 1964

Greek Cypriots Remove Strongholds

Pres. Makarios announced Apr. 21, 1965 that Greek Cypriot armed posts and road checks would be removed in the districts of Paphos, Limassol and Larraca in the western and southeastern part of the island. Greek Cypriot military strongpoints were to remain in Nicosia, where the Turkish Cypriot movement had been restricted for the previous 6 days. Vice Pres. Fazil Kutchuk Apr. 22 assailed Makarios' announcement as "an attempt to cover up the magnitude of the inhuman treatment to which the Turkish Cypriot community is being subjected at the hands of the Greek Cypriots."

The Cyprus government Apr. 15 imposed a ban on the movement of Turkish Cypriots in and out of Nicosia but lifted the ban May 3. The blockade had been instituted after a Turkish Cypriot Apr. 15 had fired at a Greek Cypriot shop owner after being caught in his store. No one was injured. Pres. Makarios lifted the ban on Turkish Cypriot traffic in Nicosia after the UN commander of the Nicosia zone, Brig. Bruce MacDonald of Canada, had reached agreement with Kutchuk May 2 on UN inspection of the empty stores.

UNFICYP Extended for Longer Periods

The UN Security Council June 15 unanimously approved a recommendation by UN Secy. Gen. U Thant to extend the life of the UN peace-keeping force in Cyprus (UNFICYP) for another 6 months — from June 26, 1965 through Dec. 26. UNFICYP's term previously had been extended 4 times for 3-month periods. But Thant asked for the longer extension for reasons of economy and efficiency. Immediately after the vote, British delegate Lord Caradon announced that Britain would maintain its soldiers in UNFICYP and contribute an additional $1 million for the force's upkeep. U.S. delegate Francis T. Plimpton said the U.S.' financial assistance to the force would continue at about its current level. The Security Council Dec. 17 unanimously approved the extension of UNFICYP's term for another 6 months — from

Dec. 26 through June 26, 1966. The force then totaled 5,766 men.
(The U.S. Dec. 13 had promised more funds for UNFICYP. The
U.S. thus far had contributed $15,800,000. 41 other countries had
given $35 million.)

UN Takes Up Electoral Reforms

The UN Security Council convened Aug. 3, 1965 to consider
a Turkish charge that electoral reforms adopted by the Cyprus
government July 23 were unconstitutional and violated the rights
of the island's Turkish Cypriot minority. After a week's debate
the Council adjourned without taking definitive action. It merely
approved (Aug. 10) by unanimous vote a resolution drafted by
Bolivia, the Ivory Coast, the Netherlands, Jordan, Malaysia and
Uruguay that: (a) took note of U Thant's recent statements on
Cyprus; (b) reaffirmed the Council's basic resolution on Cyprus of
Mar. 4, 1964; (c) appealed to all sides "in conformity with the
above [basic] resolution, to avoid any action which is likely to
worsen the situation."

The electoral reforms approved by the Cyprus House of
Representatives July 23 extended the terms of Pres. Makarios
and of the House's Greek Cypriot members (which were to expire
in August) but virtually dismissed Vice Pres. Fazil Kutchuk, the
Turkish Cypriot community leader, by not extending his term.
The reforms also replaced the separate Greek and Turkish Cypriot voting rolls with a common electoral roll. House Pres.
Glafkos Clerides had said July 22 that his government no longer
recognized the legal status of Kutchuk and of the 3 Turkish Cypriot cabinet ministers who had been replaced by Greeks. Clerides
told the 3 ministers they would be permitted to attend the July 23
session only if they recognized all laws passed by the House since
Dec. 1963. But they refused to accept these conditions and stayed
away from the meeting. Clerides said the House's Turkish members, who had been absent since 1963, would continue to be
recognized until national elections were held. The legislators had
been boycotting the House on the ground that Cyprus was in a
state of civil war.

In a report to the Security Council July 29, U Thant said that Cyprus' new electoral laws "have increased tension in the island." He cited Turkish Cypriot fears that the new rules "would eliminate the constitutional rights of the Turkish members [of the House] and of their community."

In a letter to Council Pres. Platon D. Morozov requesting the emergency session, Turkish delegate Eralp charged July 30 that Cyprus' new electoral laws were "utterly void in form and substance from a constitutional point of view and are in flagrant violation of solemn agreements upon which the constitution of the Republic of Cyprus is based." Rebutting Eralp's charges, Cypriot delegate Zenon Rossides said in a letter to Morozov that the replaced voting laws, "by their abnormality and their proven unworkability, had been the origin and the main cause of the trouble and the crisis in the island." (Fighting had erupted between the Greek and Turkish Cypriots in Dec. 1963 after Pres. Makarios had proposed to reduce political guarantees to the Turkish Cypriot community and to eliminate the Turkish Cypriot veto power in the government.) Rossides also requested a Council meeting to consider charges that Turkey, in a July 27 note to the Nicosia regime, had threatened "to take military actions against Cyprus in violation of the Charter." The Turkish note to Makarios assailed the new electoral laws and warned that Ankara would take "all necessary measures" to uphold the Cyprus constitution.

Opening the Security Council debate Aug. 3, Eralp charged that the Cypriot government's ultimate aim was to annex the island to Greece "over the objections of the Turkish Cypriot community, in defiance of international treaties and in utter disregard" of the Council's resolutions and the Cyprus constitution. Eralp appealed to the Council to prevent such action. In reply, Cypriot Foreign Min. Kyprianou said that the 1959 treaties governing Cyprus' status and providing the basis for its constitution "do not exist."

UN Probes Famagusta Clash

In the wake of armed clashes Nov. 2-3, 1965 between Greek and Turkish Cypriots in Famagusta, the UN Security Council Nov. 5 appealed to all sides in the Cyprus dispute to "refrain from any action likely to worsen the situation." The Council, meeting in emergency session at the request of Turkish delegate Eralp, issued the appeal in the form of a consensus without a formal vote following debate between Eralp and the Greek and Cyprus representatives. UN Secy. Gen. U Thant said a cease-fire that had been negotiated by UN observers at the scene "was being observed." This was confirmed by the Cypriot delegate, Foreign Min. Spyros A. Kyprianou.

Shortly before the fighting started Greek Cypriots had erected new coastal gun positions around Famagusta, a municipality held by Turkish Cypriots. A report on the clashes circulated by Thant said that the Turkish Cypriots feared the guns would be turned against them. The fighting had erupted Nov. 2 when Turkish Cypriots apparently opened fire on a Greek Cypriot National Guard force that had started to patrol an area near the Famagusta suburb of Skharia. The Greek Cypriot force captured a school building and an apartment house that the government claimed had been used by Turkish Cypriots to fire on guard units. The Turkish Cypriots claimed that the guard had planned to capture the 2 points to dominate the entrance to the city.

Enosis Affirmed as Greek & Cypriot Goal

Cypriot Pres. Makarios had declared in Nicosia Apr. 4, 1965 that *enosis* "continues to be the goal of the Cypriot people's struggle." "There can be no other victory," he said, "than a realization of the people's national aspiration" of union with Greece. Makarios conferred with Greek Premier George Papandreou in Athens May 6-8. A joint communique issued May 8 said the 2 leaders had "confirmed the desire of the 2 governments to persevere in an effort to preserve peaceful and normal conditions on the island"; "self-determination in accordance with the principles of the UN Charter remains always our steady policy." The communique made no mention of a reported rejection May 8 by the Crown Council (composed of Papandreou and former Greek premiers) of a Makarios plan calling for Cyprus' unilateral proclamation of *enosis* and for Greek support of such a stand regardless of Turkey's reaction to it. Papandreou was said to have told the council that he favored *enosis* but only through peaceful negotiation with Turkey.

The Cyprus question was discussed in Athens again Jan. 29-Feb. 1, 1966 by Makarios and the new Greek premier, Stephanos Stephanopoulos, and by other Greek and Cypriot officials. A joint statement made public Feb. 2 announced Greek and Greek Cypriot rejection of any proposed solution that would not entail *enosis* or that provided for "direct or indirect partition" of the island between Greek and Turkish Cypriot communities.

Turkish Premier Suleyman Demrel declared Feb. 4 that Turkey would not "accept *enosis,* nor shall we allow Greek oppression of the Turkish Cypriot community in Cyprus." Turkey Feb. 5 sent the Greek government a sharp note protesting the Athens talks. Turkish Foreign Min. Ihsan Sabri Caglayangil declared in parliament Feb. 7: "The question of Cyprus has taken the appearance of leading Turkey to war at a moment she does not wish, and in spite of Turkey's wanting peace more than anyone else."

UN Secy. Gen. U Thant announced Mar. 4 that he had issued new instructions Mar. 2 to his personal representative in Cyprus, Carlos A. Bernardes to seek a solution of the Cyprus dispute. Thant suggested that Bernardes attempt to bring about "discussions, at any level, of problems and issues of either a purely local or broader nature." Thant suggested that Bernardes use his "good offices and make such approaches to the parties, in or outside the island, as may seem to you to be likely to be productive." Thant's new action had been accepted in advance by the 4 governments directly involved in the dispute — Cyprus, Greece, Turkey and Britain.

UNFICYP Beset by Deficit

UN Secy. Gen. U Thant called attention to the operational deficit of the UN Force in Cyprus as the UN Security Council Mar. 16, 1966 approved the extension of UNFICYP's term for another 3 months from Mar. 26 to June 26, 1966. The Council's resolution urged all interested parties "to act with the utmost restraint and to make determined efforts with a view to achieving the objectives of the Security Council": to establish peace between the feuding Greek and Turkish Cypriot communities.

British delegate Lord Caradon responded to Thant's plea for more funds by pledging $1 million for UNFICYP's upkeep for the next 3 months. The Soviet delegate based his acceptance of UNFICYP's extension on the continued voluntary payments for the force. Thant had been holding talks since Mar. 1 with British, Greek, Turkish and Cypriot officials on UNFICYP's critical fund shortage. In a letter dated Mar. 24 and made public Mar. 29, Thant disclosed that UNFICYP's deficit totaled $2,686,860 and that the force required an additional $5,700,000 in operating funds for the new 3-month period through June 26. Thant pleaded for funds from UN member states as well as voluntary contributions from non-member nations that maintained permanent observers at the UN. Australia Mar. 29 pledged $75,000 for the period ended Mar. 26. Switzerland had pledged $130,000 in a note to Thant Mar. 7 (made public Mar. 11); the Berne government also offered its good offices to help resolve Cyprus' political deadlock.

Ireland informed Thant Apr. 1 that it would withdraw its 518 troops from UNFICYP's 4,768-man force Apr. 18. Ireland had warned Thant of the projected withdrawal Mar. 24 if the Dublin government were not assured of repayment for expenses incurred. A UN spokesman said Thant was unable to guarantee reimbursement. The Finnish government was reported Apr. 2 to have decided to keep its troops in UNFICYP at Thant's request. Finland, Denmark and Sweden had warned Thant Mar. 25 that their continued troop contribution beyond June 26 depended on achieving political progress in Cyprus.

The Security Council June 16 unanimously approved the extension of UNFICYP's term for another 6 months — until Dec. 26. The Council voted unanimously Dec. 15 to extend

UNFICYP operations for an additional 6 months ending June 26, 1967. The resolution expressed hope that "sufficient progress towards the solution by then will make possible a withdrawal or substantial reduction of the force."

Greek Government Dispute

Greek Foreign Min. Elias Tsirimokos resigned Apr. 11, 1966 in protest against his government's Cyprus policy. Ioannis Tsirimokos, his nephew and a pro-government deputy in parliament, withdrew his support of the government the same day. Welfare Min. Mimis Galinos resigned April 12. Retired Vice Adm. Ioannis Toumbas, who had been interior minister in the Papandreou government, was sworn in May 11 as Greece's new foreign minister. John Glavanis replaced Toumbas as interior minister, and Constantine Maris succeeded Glavanis as industry minister. Ioannis Yamas simultaneously became communications minister to replace Ioannis Yannopoulos, who received the public health portfolio.

The Apr. 11-12 resignations from the Greek government were precipitated by Greek Premier Stephanos Stephanopoulos' support of Lt. Gen. George Grivas, Greek-appointed defense minister of Cyprus, in his feud with Pres. Makarios. Makarios, supported by Tsirimokos, had asked the Greek government to revoke Grivas' command of the 11,000-man Cypriot national guard and thereby to restrict his authority to the 10,000 Greek troops stationed on the island. (Makarios charged that Grivas was trying to use the national guard to stage a military coup and was plotting his assassination.) Tsirimokos and Galinos resigned after Stephanopoulos and Defense Min Stavros Costopoulos had rejected Makarios' request.

The resignations caused Stephanopoulos temporarily to lose his majority in parliament (he had controlled 152 votes out of 300). The majority was restored when 2 members of ex-Premier Papandreou's opposition Center Union party (CU) defected Apr. 15 and Galinos returned to the cabinet Apr. 18. Stephanopoulos denied charges that the government had offered bribes of $166,000 and cabinet posts to opposition deputies for their support. The CU Apr. 19 tabled motions of "no confidence" that would have censured the government not only for its Cyprus policy but for all aspects of its activities, including the bribery charges. The government narrowly defeated the motions by 151-147 vote.

Nicosia's Turkish Quarter Blockaded; New Fighting

The Cypriot government imposed a blockade of the Turkish quarter of Nicosia June 1-4, 1966 in reprisal for 2 explosions outside the guarded zone. The blasts were attributed to Turkish Cypriots. The blockade was reimposed June 20 for no apparent reason. Turkey warned Greece that unless the Nicosia restrictions were removed by June 23, Ankara would undertake "countermeasures." Athens relayed the warning to the Cypriot government. UN officials in Cyprus informed U Thant, who in turn urged Pres. Makarios June 22 to lift the blockade. Makarios complied June 23.

Thant had reported to the UN Security Council June 11 that tension between the Greek and Turkish communities had been on the rise because of shooting incidents and the building of fortifications by both sides. Thant said that his personal representative in Cyprus, Carlos A. Bernardes, had made no progress in his mediation efforts. Bernardes had discussed with Greek, Turkish and Cypriot officials in May an informal Thant plan that would have suspended the 1959 Cyprus independence treaties for 3 to 5 years, after which negotiations would start for a final solution of the dispute. Under Thant's plan: an independent Cypriot regime would be guaranteed by the U.S., France, Britain and the USSR; the rights of the Turkish minority in Cyprus would be guaranteed by the UN Security Council; Greek and Turkish troops would be removed from the island.

Fresh outbreaks of fighting between Greek and Turkish Cypriots took place in July-August, 1967. Armed members of the 2 communities had exchanged fire for 3 hours July 20 at Ayios Theodoros in the eastern part of the island. No casualties were reported. Heavy firing broke out again in the same area July 29. More than 1,000 shots were fired before UN observers arranged a cease-fire. 2 Greek Cypriots were wounded by snipers the same day in Kophinou, 2 miles away. 2 Turkish Cypriots were shot to death Aug. 6 outside the Turkish Cypriot village of Kouroukas. 2 Greek Cypriots were arrested as suspects. About 10 Greek and Turkish Cypriots had been reported slain in the area in earlier clashes.

In a move to reduce tension between the 2 Cypriot communities, the Cyprus government Sept. 2, 1967 announced plans for "absolute freedom of movement" in the southwest part of the island. The plan called for leaving all armed posts and roadblocks unguarded. The government said that if the plan succeeded, security measures would be relaxed in other parts of Cyprus.

Greek-Turkish Talks

Greece and Turkey agreed May 18, 1966 that their foreign ministers should meet to negotiate a "peaceful and agreed settlement" of the Cyprus controversy. The talks were made possible after both sides had approved the idea of not posing prior conditions. The foreign ministers held their first informal discussions during the NATO meeting in Brussels in June. The Greek and Turkish governments announced later that further bilateral talks would be held privately in an undisclosed neutral capital.

The direct Greek-Turkish talks proposed by Ankara in 1965 were held Sept. 9-10, 1967 but no progress was reported. Greek Premier Constantine V. Kollias, Turkish Premier Suleyman Demirel and their aides met in Kesan, Turkey Sept. 9 and in Alexandroupolis, Greece Sept. 10. A joint communique issued at the conclusion of the conference said both premiers had "acknowledged the fact that the resumption of good and cordial relations between their 2 countries depended in the first instance on an equitable solution" of the Cyprus problem. "They agreed therefore to continue ... the exploration of possibilities for a rapprochement of their viewpoints on this issue."

Clash Threatens Greek-Turkish War

Communal fighting on Cyprus Nov. 15-16, 1967 threatened to escalate into war between Greece and Turkey. The Ankara government warned Greece that its forces would invade Cyprus to protect the Turkish Cypriot minority there unless Greece withdrew its troops from the island. Turkey backed its threat by mobilizing army, air and naval units and massing forces at the Turkish port of Mersin, 80 miles north of Cyprus.

Successful international efforts to head off a Greek-Turkish clash were undertaken by a special U.S. envoy, Cyrus R. Vance, by the UN and by NATO, of which Greece and Turkey were members.

The communal fighting erupted Nov. 15 in the southern villages of Ayios Theodoros (mixed population) and Kophinou (all Turkish) and caused the death of 24 Turkish Cypriots and 4 Greek Cypriots. The first clash took place when a force of Greek Cypriot police led by National Guardsmen attempted to resume the patrolling of the Turkish area of Ayios Theodoros, where a patrol had entered Nov. 14 but had been warned by Turkish Cypriots not to return. On approaching the village Nov. 15, the patrol was stopped by a tractor on the road and was fired on when it tried to remove it. The Greek Cypriot force returned the fire. The fighting quickly spread to neighboring Kophinou, 2 miles away, where another Greek Cypriot patrol was fired on. The violence ended early Nov. 16.

A communique issued by the Cypriot government Nov. 15 said the National Guard had "neutralized all resistance" in both villages.

A spokesman for UNFICYP said Nov. 15 that the UN had protested to the Nicosia regime against interfering with UN forces in the area. The note said the National Guard had disarmed UN troops, seized UN weapons and disabled UN radio equipment.

A statement by the Turkish Cypriot community Nov. 16 charged that (a) the attack on Ayios Theodoros and Kophinou was an all-out military operation involving 3,000 Greek Cypriot troops, 40 armored vehicles and heavy artillery, and (b) the Greek Cypriots had fired indiscriminately on the inhabitants of the villages and had broken into homes, where they looted "everything they found in a frenzy of hatred."

Turkey's first reaction to the crisis came Nov. 16 when it warned the U.S., Britain and the UN that it would intervene militarily unless the shooting stopped at Ayios Theodoros and Kophinou. The Ankara regime alerted its air and ground forces, and Turkish naval units sailed for Mediterranean waters off Turkey's southern coast. Turkey Nov. 17 started air force reconnaissance flights over Cyprus.

The U.S. Nov. 16 appealed to the Greek and Turkish Cypriot communities and to King Constantine of Greece for restraint. UN Secy. Gen. U Thant had discussed the crisis at separate meetings with the UN delegates from Greece, Turkey and Cyprus Nov. 15.

Turkey was reported to have called on Greece Nov. 17 to remove its troops from Cyprus. A note delivered to Athens was said to have included these other demands: removal from Cyprus of Gen. George Grivas, commander of the Cyprus National Guard and of the Greek troops on the island (Grivas left for Athens Nov. 19 for consultation with Greek government officials); compensation for the deaths and damage in Ayios Theodoros; guarantee that similar incidents would not recur; the lifting of restrictions against Turkish Cypriots currently confined to their communal enclaves. (An estimated 8,000-12,000 Greek soldiers were stationed on Cyprus although only 950 were authorized under the 1960 London and Zurich agreements guaranteeing Cyprus' independence. Turkey had several hundred more troops in Cyprus than the 650 permitted.)

Greece replied Nov. 22 and reportedly rejected the Turkish demands. The delivery of the reply was announced by Greek Foreign Min. Panayotis Pipinelis (who had been appointd to his post Nov. 20). Pipinelis denied that the Turkish note was an ultimatum. "Our main concern," he said, "is to ease tension." Turkish Foreign Min. Ishan Sabri Caglayangil also affirmed that Turkey had put no time limit on its demand for the removal of Greek troops from Cyprus.

Pres. Makarios said in a broadcast Nov. 24: Turkey "may force war on us. Whether the war which threatens . . . will be avoided or not does not depend on us."

Action to Avert Greek-Turkish Conflict

In a coordinated effort to avert war between Greece and
Turkey, U.S., UN and NATO representatives met with Greek,
Turkish and Cypriot officials in their respective capitals Nov. 23-
28. The envoys were: ex-U.S. Deputy Defense Secy. Cyrus R.
Vance, appointed by Pres. Johnson Nov. 22 as his special aide in
the crisis; UN Undersecy. (for special political affairs) Jose Rolz-
Bennett, representing UN Secy. Gen. U Thant; NATO Secy.
Gen. Manlio Brosio.

Vance met with Greek and Turkish leaders in Athens and
Ankara Nov. 23-28. He was reported Nov. 27 to have proposed
this formula to resolve the dispute: Greece and Turkey would
remove from Cyprus those troops not authorized by the 1960
independence accord; Greece and Turkey would reaffirm their
previous pledges to respect the independence and integrity of
Cyprus; Turkey would demobilize the troops it had massed at the
start of the crisis; the Cypriot police force would be reorganized
by or under the supervision of the 4,500-man UN Force in
Cyprus (UNFICYP).

A plan proposed by Canadian Prime Min. Lester B. Pearson
was presented to Greek Foreign Min. Pipinelis Nov. 22 by the
U.S., British and Canadian ambassadors in Athens. The plan
called for a reduction of Greek and Turkish troops in Cyprus, an
expansion of UNFICYP's powers and the barring of Gen.
George Grivas from Cyprus. Pipinelis summoned the 3 ambassadors Nov. 23 and reportedly expressed partial approval of the
Canadian proposal.

Brosio and Rolz-Bennett met with Greek officials in Athens
Nov. 26, conferred with each other and then left for Ankara and
Nicosia respectively. Pres. Makarios was reported Nov. 27 to
have told Rolz-Bennett that he favored (a) the withdrawal of
Greek and Turkish troops from Cyprus with a view toward the
island's eventual demilitarization, and (b) the retention of
UNFICYP troops.

UN Urges Restraint

The UN Security Council Nov. 25 unanimously approved a resolution calling on all sides in the Cyprus dispute to exercise restraint to avert war. U Thant had issued similar pleas Nov. 22 and 24. The Council's resolution, adopted by consensus without a vote, requested that all interested parties "assist and cooperate in keeping peace and arriving at a permanent settlement."

The Council had been called into emergency session Nov. 24 at the request of Zenon Rossides, chief delegate of Cyprus. Rossides urged the Council to adopt a resolution "to protect the territorial integrity, the sovereignty and political independence of Cyprus from ... invasion by Turkey." Turkish delegate Orhan Eralp charged that the only threat to peace in Cyprus was "the presence of the illegal Greek army of occupation, which has been brought to the island surreptitiously and with the collusion of the Greek Cypriot administration." Dimitri Bitsios, chief Greek delegate, asserted that "the unleashing of aggression" by Turkey "is imminent."

Thant Nov. 22 had expressed concern over the "military preparations, the movement of forces and threatening statements" in the Cyprus dispute. Thant's views were outlined in parallel messages to Cypriot Pres. Makarios, Greek Premier Constantine V. Kollias and Turkish Premier Suleyman Demirel. Thant urged the 3 leaders "to avoid any action that could precipitate a new outbreak of hostilities and to exercise the utmost restraint in the present explosive circumstances." He informed them of his decision to send Rolz-Bennett to Cyprus, Greece and Turkey "to assist them in all possible ways to reduce the present tension." In a 2d message to Makarios, Kollias and Demirel, Thant Nov. 24 stressed the need for the removal of Greek and Turkish troops from Cyprus. Thant said "tensions could be eased and the imminent threat of war removed by ... [an] effort by the 3 parties directly concerned to ... arrange for a substantial reduction [and eventual total withdrawal] of non-Cypriot forces now in hostile confrontation" on Cyprus. Thant suggested that the withdrawal could be carried out in phases and thus "make possible the positive demilitarization of Cyprus." He offered his "assistance in carrying out such a program and in continuing to help maintain quiet."

Greece & Turkey Agree on Troop Removal

Greece and Turkey Dec. 3, 1967 signed an internationally-mediated agreement resolving the immediate issues that had threatened to cause war between them.

Cyprus as well as Greece and Turkey informed UN Secy. Gen. U Thant in separate messages Dec. 3 that all 3 governments involved had accepted the pact. Their messages were in response to a fresh peace appeal issued by Thant earlier on Dec. 3. Cyrus R. Vance, Pres. Johnson's special envoy, who had been meeting with the interested parties in Athens, Ankara and Nicosia since Nov. 23, was reported to have drawn up Thant's plea after the Turkish and Cypriot governments had reached an impasse over Ankara's demands for disarming the Greek Cypriot National Guard. Pres. Makarios had insisted that disarming the guard (provided for in the Greek-Turkish agreement) must be deferred pending negotiations dealing with the demilitarization of Cyprus. Thant's Dec. 3 appeal dealt with all aspects of the Greek-Turkish agreement except the question of the National Guard.

The Greek-Turkish pact called for: (a) the removal from Cyprus within 45 days of all Greek and Turkish troops not authorized under the 1960 Cyprus independence accord; (b) the dismantling within 45 days of all Greek and Turkish war preparations that had precipitated the crisis; (c) the disarming of all local military forces on Cyprus, particularly the Greek Cypriot National Guard; (d) the expansion of the 4,500-man UN Force to prevent further communal clashes between Greek and Turkish Cypriots.

Amplifying his positive response to Thant's Dec. 3 peace plea, Makarios Dec. 4 sent Thant a 2d message in which he suggested that the UN Security Council provide guarantees against military intervention in Cyprus. Makarios qualified his acceptance of UNFICYP's proposed expansion by declaring that "enlargement" of the UN force's "mandate" would have to be considered by the Security Council "with due regard to the sovereignty" of Cyprus.

In compliance with the 3-nation agreement, Greece began to remove troops from Cyprus, and 400 soldiers sailed from Famagusta Dec. 8.

(About 500 dependents of U.S. government officials on Cyprus had started to leave the island for Beirut at the height of the crisis Nov. 23. The American families began to return to Cyprus Dec. 8.)

Vance returned to Washington Dec. 4 and met with Pres. Johnson Dec. 5. The President then said that war over Cyprus had been averted but that international efforts must be undertaken "with a sense of new urgency" to resolve the basic issues of the dispute. 2 other diplomats who had participated with Vance in coordinated efforts to head off a Greek-Turkish clash had left Athens Nov. 30 to go back to their respective posts. They were NATO Secy. Gen. Manlio Brosio, who returned to Brussels, and UN Undersecy. Jose Rolz-Bennett, who went back to New York.

Turkish Cypriots Form 'Transitional' Regime

Turkish Cypriot leaders Dec. 28, 1967 formed a "transitional administration" that was to have "jurisdiction over all Turks living in Turkish zones" on Cyprus. The regime went into operation Dec. 29. The Cypriot and Greek governments protested the move.

The new governing body including all officials of the former Turkish Cypriot leadership, was an 11-member Executive Council headed by ex-Vice Pres Fazil Kutchuk. Exiled Turkish Cypriot leader Rauf Denktash was named 2d in command. Attending the meeting establishing the council were 2 Turkish government officials — Zeki Kuneralp, secretary general of the Turkish Foreign Ministry, and Suat Bilge, the ministry's chief legal adviser.

Pres. Makarios Dec. 29 assailed the Turkish Cypriot action as a "flagrantly unlawful" move that undermined the good offices of UN Secy. Gen. U Thant, whose intercession had led to the agreement that had averted a clash over Cyprus between Greece and Turkey. Makarios asserted that the presence of Turkish government officials at the Turkish Cypriot meeting

Dec. 28 "constitutes an inadmissible and provocative intervention by Turkey in the internal affairs of Cyprus."

A Greek Foreign Ministry statement Dec. 29 said that the Turkish Cypriots' establishment of a separate administration in Cyprus "creates a very serious situation." Referring to the Dec. 1 Greek-Turkish pact, the ministry said that "by their action the Turks evidently want to prejudice such a solution in order to impose their own."

The Cypriot government Dec. 30 declared Zeki Runeralp *persona non grata* and asked him to leave Cyprus because of "his provocative statements and interference in the internal affairs of Cyprus." Runeralp left for Turkey that day.

Cypriot Acting Foreign Min. Andreas Arouzos Dec. 30 urged the ambassadors to Cyprus from the U.S., Britain, the Soviet Union, France, the UAR and Yugoslavia not to visit members of the new Turkish Cypriot administration. To do so, he said, would be tantamount to recognition of the Turkish Cypriot Executive Council and contrary to the ambassadors' accreditation with the Cypriot government.

Cypriot Foreign Min. Spyros A. Kyprianou conferred with Thant Dec. 29 and said Dec. 30 that he had told the secretary general that the creation of a formal Turkish Cypriot administration did not affect the political situation in Cyprus because it could not be implemented. Kyprianou, however, said he had accused Turkey of colluding with the Turkish Cypriots in defying a Dec. 22 UN Security Council resolution that had called on all parties in the Cyprus dispute to work for peace and had extended UNFICYP for 3 more months, to Mar. 26, 1968.

Turkish Amb.-to-UN Orhan Eralp conferred with Thant Dec. 30 and assured him that the formation of the Turkish Cypriot Executive Council did not represent a real change in the situation. Asserting that "it was an entirely internal matter for Cyprus," Eralp said he had told Thant that the establishment of the Executive Council would assist him by providing him with "a responsible group to deal with that represented the Turkish community" in Cyprus.

The Security Council's Dec. 22 action on Cyprus had been approved unanimously without debate. The Council, which had been discussing the Cyprus problem since Dec. 8, did not extend Thant's authority for negotiating the dispute. It merely accepted his Dec. 3 offer of his good offices incorporated in peace pleas sent to Greece, Turkey and Cyprus. Thant, in a report filed with the Security Council Dec. 11, had recommended UNFICYP's extension for 3 to 6 months beyond the Dec. 26 expiration date. Referring to the Ayios Theodoros clash of Nov. 15-16 that had precipitated the latest Greek-Turkish crisis, Thant charged that the Greek Cypriot National Guard had used "disproportionate force" in trying to restore order in the mixed village when UNFICYP observers were about to effect a long-range settlement. Thant blamed both Turkish Cypriots and the National Guard for having denied UNFICYP teams "freedom of movement" on 52 occasions, on 16 of which "the use of force was threatened." The tense Cyprus situation had been partly exacerbated, Thant said, when the Cypriot House of Representatives June 11 approved a law permitting non-Cyprus residents (mainland Greeks) to join the National Guard.

In a report filed with the Security Council Jan. 4, 1968, Thant complained that the Turkish Cypriot leadership had given no official reason for establishing the "transitional administration" and had not explained the scope of its operations. Thant said he had been told that the action was aimed only at making the administration of the Turkish community more workable. A statement issued by the Turkish mission at the UN Jan. 4 said that the Turkish Cypriot community had undertaken the move because "it was necessary to reorganize its administrative arrangements and announced the adoption of a set of regulations to give this effect to this reorganization."

Makarios Reelected President

Archbishop Makarios was reelected Feb. 25, 1968 to a 2d 5-year term as president of Cyprus. He received 220,911 votes to 8,577 for his only rival, Dr. Takis Evdokas, 40. More than 90% of the 247,000 eligible Greek Cypriot voters cast ballots. (Turkish

Cypriots elected the vice president.) Evdokas, a psychiatrist, was supported in the election campaign by an extremist front that advocated *enosis*. Makarios was sworn in Feb. 29.

Makarios had first been elected president in 1959. His term had expired in 1965 but was extended twice by the Greek Cypriot parliament because of the crisis caused by the continued communal strife. Makarios had called the election Jan. 12 to seek a new mandate in view of the new developments in the Cyprus problem — a breakdown in talks between Greece and Turkey and Greece's decision to withdraw from Cyprus all troops not authorized under the 1960 Cyprus independence accord. The withdrawal of 7,000 such Greek troops was completed Jan. 16.

The Greek-Turkish impasse took place at UN headquarters in New York, where Secy. Gen. U Thant sought to resolve the dispute arising from the decision by the Turkish Cypriots to establish a "transitional administration." Turkey had insisted that Thant's role in the Cyprus-Greek-Turkish talks should be restricted to the easing of immediate tensions and not be used to pave the way for a general settlement of the Cyprus dispute. This view was challenged by Cyprus and Greece, which advocated that Thant be authorized to work out an overall agreement. Zenon Rossides, Cyprus' representative at the UN, demanded Feb. 10 that Turkey make clear whether it still claimed the right to intervene militarily in Cyprus to protect the Turkish Cypriot community. Rossides' note, handed to U Thant and circulated to all UN member states, protested that an earlier letter from Orhan Eralp, Turkey's UN delegate, had evaded the question of the right of intervention. Turkey had insisted that it had the right to use force to come to the aid of the Turkish Cypriots under the 1960 independence accord.

UN Peace Force Again Extended

The UN Security Council voted unanimously Mar. 18, 1968 to extend the UN force in Cyprus for 3 more months — to June 26. An accompanying resolution urged "the utmost restraint" on the Greek and Turkish communities in Cyprus. By Council votes June 18 and Dec. 10, UNFICYP was given additional extensions — of 3 months and of 6 months, respectively.

In a report to the Council Mar. 11, U Thant had said there had been "a significant lessening of tensions" in Cyprus since Nov. 1967, when Greece and Turkey had threatened to go to war over the island dispute. Thant attributed the more peaceful atmosphere to Pres. Makarios' decision Mar. 8 to remove all Greek police and road blocks in the Nicosia area and thus give Turkish Cypriots freedom of movement for the first time in more than 4 years. The barriers that had divided the Greek and Turkish sectors in the capital were also removed.

The Security Council voted unanimously June 10, 1969 to extend UNFICYP's operations for 6 more months, until Dec. 15. U Thant had requested the extension in a report to the Council June 4. Thant said the presence of the UN force was not enough to maintain peace between the island's Greek and Turkish Cypriot communities. He said a political solution must be reached to avert open warfare. Thant confirmed that Greek and Turkish officials had been holding secret negotiations in a effort to settle the dispute, but he warned that "the passage of too much time may hamper rather than facilitate the settlement of the Cyprus problem." The UN Force was subsequently extended for periodic 6-month intervals through through June 15, 1970, at about the time this volume went to press.